"Division in the church is an affront to Christ and a hindrance to a lost world. Christians, of all people, should be instruments of peace. Jack Reese is candid but kind in calling for Christians to be Christian in their treatment of one another. Without a doubt, this is the best book I've ever read on healing the wounds of division in the church."

—**Victor Knowles**, President, Peace on Earth Ministries, Joplin, Missouri

"Jack Reese charts a spiritual journey from brokenness and strife to wholeness and peace. It is a demanding journey—one that engages both mind and heart—but it is a road worth traveling."

—**Jerry Rushford**, Professor of Church History, Pepperdine University, Malibu, California

"Jack Reese anguishes over the fragmented state of the Church and appeals for mutual respect among Christians who differ. He recognizes the place of baptism in becoming a Christian. He calls us to actively seek peace through kindness, gentleness and humility. However, when dealing with issues such as instrumental music and greater inclusion of women in leadership in Christian assemblies, it seems too simplistic to say, "Over this issue the church must not divide." When practices violate the conscientious convictions of worshippers, they must assemble separately, or compromise their convictions. These issues must be specifically discussed. So *The Body Broken* calls us to discussion. Let's heed that call."

—**Cecil May Jr.**, Dean, V. P. Black College of Biblical Studies, Faulkner University, Montgomery, Alabama

"The central plea of this book is simple: we ought to be able to talk to each other. If these insightful, well-crafted words can help us do that, they'll be an invaluable gift to the church, for it's so much easier to stereotype, demonize, and criticize than to listen, encourage, and agree to disagree."

—**Mike Cope**, Preaching Minister, Highland Church of Christ, Abilene, Texas

"Two thousand years ago the Apostle Paul wrote of Christ's broken body, believers choosing sides, even favorite apostles. In what reads like a sermon from a preacher in love with the church, Jack Reese offers up the hope that what has been the pattern of the past will not be our faith's future. What a helpful word at a time when civil discourse has ceased to be civil or true discourse."

—**Mike Graves,** Regional Minister of Preaching, Greater Kansas City Christian Church (Disciples of Christ); Professor of Homiletics and Worship, Central Baptist Theological Seminary

"I believe God's heart is broken over the fragmentation of the church. This book brought me to tears over our divisiveness. I praise God for Jack's courage, boldness, heart, and commitment to heal the body of Christ."

—**Gregg Marutzky**, Minister, DFW Church of Christ, Carrollton, Texas

THE BODY
BROKEN

JACK R. REESE

THE BODY BROKEN

EMBRACING

+HE PEACE OF CHRIS+ IN

A FRAGMEN+ED CHURCH

LEAFWOOD
PUBLISHERS

THE BODY BROKEN
Embracing the Peace of Christ in a Fragmented Church
published by Leafwood Publishers

Cover design by Greg Jackson, Jackson Design

For information:
Leafwood Publishers
Siloam Springs, AR
1-877-634-6004 (toll free)

Visit our website: www.leafwoodpublishers.com

05   06   07   08   09   10 / 7   6   5   4   3   2   1

CONTENTS

ACKNOWLEDGEMENTS

I am grateful to many people whose contributions to this project have been substantial. My wife has been my most important conversation partner from the beginning. Jeanene, who has both theological training and ministry experience in addition to knowing me better than anyone, offered significant help at key moments. Because we work so closely together, it is sometimes hard to know whose ideas come from whom. On more than a few occasions, her suggestions were exactly what I needed. Her fingerprints can be discerned throughout this document. She is a visionary thinker, a talented teacher, a faithful partner, a person of peace, and a gift to me from God.

I am also grateful for Jeanene's thoughtful work on the study guide. She, along with my friend Gary Holloway, have provided an extremely useful set of reflections, study questions, and cases that should make the book useful for churches and church leaders.

It has been wonderful having adult children whose insights are much deeper than my own. I have leaned substantially on them in the writing of this book. The very first feedback I received from anyone came from our daughter Jocelyn and her husband, Mark Wiebe. They read an early draft of a chapter and provided a valuable critique that has guided me for the rest of my writing. They also gave me the last feedback I received over the book, causing me to re-think several conclusions and re-write several sections. Our eldest child, Jessica, and her husband, Jonathan Goudeau, have also been faithful conversation partners in this project. Jessica's editorial skills are well beyond most professors I ever had in graduate school, but her red marks have always been accompanied by words of affirmation and support. The final product is significantly better because of her attention and care. Our son, Jay, was especially helpful in providing feedback for a section in chapter 2 concerning why some are leaving Churches of Christ. His care and concern for the church as well as his insights into his own generation have been very useful.

Derran Reese has been my graduate assistant during this project. He is my nephew but is as dear as a son. He has read every version of the manuscript meticulously and has made numerous suggestions concerning form, style, and content. His perspectives concerning ministry and culture are beyond his years. His theological and exegetical insights have been invaluable. The book is substantially better because of his many contributions.

This book is possible only because I was granted a sabbatical to write it. Dwayne VanRheenen, my provost, and Royce Money, my president, not only allowed the time away but encouraged me throughout. They are both committed churchmen and men of character and integrity. Don Crisp, the chairman of our board, has also encouraged me from the beginning of the project.

Two families offered their ranch homes so that I could write in privacy. I am grateful to Doug and Nan Smith of Nashville whose place just south of Abilene became my home away from home for many weeks. They care greatly about the topic of this book and have been sources of encouragement for years. Rip and Liz Boss manage the Smith ranch near View. I enjoyed my conversations with them about the hills and valleys nearby, about their family, and about their love for the church. I also appreciate my dear friend Barbara Bates Johnston of San Antonio and her daughters Deanie Dampier, Kim Simpson, and Lisa Stamps for the use of their ranch home near Hunt, Texas. They are lifelong friends and dear partners in the faith. Some of my greatest inspirations occurred as I looked out their picture window watching deer and wild turkeys walk across a nearby meadow just beyond Kelly Creek.

Several friends provided special opportunities for retreat during the writing. I am indebted to Jim and Mignon Martin, Jack and Laura Riehl, and Kent Bogle. I have also received personal support and encouragement from Mike Rock, Dan and Karen Allen, David and Vonnie Perry, Josh Ross, Trey Shirley, Mark Hadley, Luke Norsworthy, and Steve Sargent.

Many people have read part or all of the manuscript at various stages of my writing. All have made helpful suggestions. Readers include Randy Harris, Gregg Marutzky, Ken Cukrowski, James Thompson, Doug Foster, Jeff Childers, Dan McVey, Larry Henderson, and Jerry Taylor. Their critiques have been very helpful. Many of the best ideas came from them. I am responsible, however, for any mistakes in style or content. I am grateful for Carolyn Thompson, who read the final manuscript with great care. My parents, Leon and Iris Reese, also made several suggestions that I incorporated in the final version. I am especially grateful to Pam Hadfield who has been both my personal assistant and an important conversation partner in this project.

Finally, I extend my deepest appreciation to Leonard Allen of Leafwood Publishers. Leonard has been my friend since 1978. Through the years he has taught me more than any teacher I have had, not just about theology and history, but about life and about Christian relationships. In this project, he has been far more than an editor or publisher. His insights have been penetrating. His council has been wise. Those who know the story of our friendship understand something of what it means for me to work with Leonard on this project. He is a man of peace. God has truly been gracious to us.

May God grant us all the courage to embrace the peace of Christ to the benefit of our churches and for the sake of his kingdom.

Jack Reese
Abilene, Texas
1 March 2005

INTRODUCTION

We suffer the failures and weaknesses of our churches.
Yet such afflictions are none other than the suffering that
shapes the church into the body of our Lord.

—R. R. Reno

The church faces threats that imperil its witness and its future. For half a century at least, buffeted by profound cultural changes and ecclesial conflicts, many Christians have experienced no small measure of anxiety and fear. Considering all that has happened, this response is not surprising. Things are not what they used to be. In substantial ways, the future will not look like the past, at least as many have idealized the past. As a consequence, public rhetoric in the church has grown heated. Even worse, in many places meaningful communication has ceased. Some are advocating further division. Others shrug at the division they believe has already occurred in fact if not in name. The church is fragmented, Christ's body broken.

For this very reason, there is cause for hope.

I do not mean to minimize the impact of the polarization we are witnessing. It is destructive and sinful. Too many congregations are impaired by gossip. Too many reputations are damaged by personal attack. Too few hearts are consumed by a desire for unity. What we are experiencing God did not intend and does not desire. Within the present circumstances, however, lie seeds of opportunity. The difficulties we face actually serve as fertile soil for the gospel. It should be clear by now that we are not capable of fixing ourselves. We are not strong enough or wise enough to repair what we have damaged. But hope is possible because in such situations God has always done his greatest work.

Moreover, because the values of the prevailing culture are increasingly hostile to the values of God's kingdom, because Christians are awakening to the social crosscurrents against which they must swim, the time is ripe for the church to become what God called it to be in the first place. We are not participants in an American civil religion. We have not retreated into a fortress against a world largely pagan. Rather, we are the very incarnation of Christ on earth, the embodiment of his suffering and a powerful agency for his redemptive work. Because we are broken, we participate in the brokenness of Christ; thus we share his power and his ministry. Therein lies our promise, and so we trust and wait.

Waiting, I must tell you, is not easy for me. Patience is not my strong suit. But I am out of alternatives. I find myself worn out by the destructive rhetoric that debilitates many churches and by the discouragement that inevitably follows. I am weary of hearing about Christians who wound each other, who know how to speak but not how to listen, who enable harmful behavior by their silence, men and women who pass on rumors and speak unkindly of others. I am discouraged by Christians who perpetuate, by action or apathy, the racial divisions that have marked our past. The church cannot continue to bear such fragmenting behavior. Nor are we able to fix it on our own. This is a time for clear thinking and compassionate behavior, for caution but also courage. The days call for humility and much prayer so that by God's power we might become a people of peace.

Though I hesitate to say so explicitly, I feel I have pursued this project less than it has pursued me. Writing this book has been for me an act of surrender. I share this not to claim that what I say here, therefore, must be true. I am too aware of human shortcomings, especially my own, to assert that. But saying nothing is no longer an option. I believe my past reticence to respond to sinful and divisive behavior has caused me at times to be complicit in the abuse that others have suffered. I am willing to risk being wrong, but I am no longer willing to risk being silent. Moreover, I believe that the brokenness of our churches and the divisive spirit that often causes it affect every Christian. I believe that until we face these challenges directly we will continue to be largely ineffective in our ministries and impotent in our Christian witness.

My church experiences, and therefore my point of reference in this book, are broadly within the Stone-Campbell Restoration Movement and specifically within a cappella Churches of Christ. I share this without defensiveness or apology. I recognize as well as anyone the flaws in this fellowship, but I believe in its greatest impulses. I share its devotion to Scripture as God's authoritative word and its commitment to baptism as the powerful and redemptive work of God. I believe in weekly participation in the Lord's Supper and affirm the high view of church that has been reflected throughout the restoration tradition. I have been profoundly shaped by this heritage and these beliefs. I write, think, worship, and live within its deepest instincts. I have been blessed immensely by those who taught me and who nurtured my faith.

At the same time, though most of the stories I have included reflect my experiences within Churches of Christ, I am very aware of readers outside that fellowship. I believe others within the Stone-Campbell heritage will find much to engage them here, especially members of the International Churches of Christ and Independent Christian Churches as well as the Christian Church (Disciples of Christ) because of what we have in common. However, because the primary focus of this work is not the unique concerns of a particular set of churches but rather a discussion of God's desires for all of us, people from outside the Stone-Campbell Restoration Movement are welcome in this dialogue. Such conversations should not be cause for fear or apprehension. Constructive dialogue among people of good will is both civil and Christian, both helpful and right.

My thesis is simple: Christians ought to be able to talk to one another. A hallmark of the church should be the ability of believers to discuss, listen, encourage, and love. We should be able to disagree without acrimony. We should be known, of all people, as instruments of peace, as agents of reconciliation. We ought to love each other so profoundly, serve each other so aggressively, listen to each other so passionately, and respond to each other so humbly, that the kingdom of God breaks in among us. That is my goal and prayer.

In large measure this work is a reflection on Christian unity. My purpose, however, is modest. I have not attempted to write a systematic or comprehensive theology of unity. This book is more narrative in nature and less technical. At the same time, while I have chosen to be intensely personal, I have tried to exercise restraint in that regard so that the narrative does not draw attention away from the larger point. My intention is to engage in conversation with the readers, to write as I talk, or at least as I preach. I want the reader to see me as a fellow struggler. My desire is that we walk side by side in this search and that, over time, a level of trust might emerge.

My overall goal, of course, is to write what is true. I want to say what God says, to do what God desires. I want the extensive discussions of biblical materials to reflect God's purposes. I have tried to do careful exegesis of every passage. Moreover, I have been conscientious about my descriptions of contemporary times and cultures. While I have sometimes been casual in approach, I have tried never to be cavalier. Beyond that I have had several specific goals for the style and tone of the book.

First, I want my language to be tender. Even though the topic and times call for boldness, I never want my language to be violent or abusive. I love the church too much to want to hurt her or any of her members. I do not want to apply bellows to hot coals of conflict. Over and over I have toned down superlatives and eliminated phrases that might cause unnecessary offense. While I am still very direct at times, I trust the reader will hear the respect with which I hold the church and the tenderness in my heart towards her.

Second, I am committed to being confessional. Throughout, I have approached these problems not as *theirs* or *yours* but as *ours*. As long as we all assume that others are guilty while our own behavior is justified, we will remain at an impasse. Such a posture is not only unfair, it is unhealthy for the church. I have witnessed spiritual abuse, to be sure, and I have been victimized by it. But I have also contributed to the church's fragmentation. I have spoken inappropriately. I have not been as careful as I should have been. I have not always listened. I have engaged in gossip. I have sinned. Out of our willingness to confess, I believe, comes the possibility of peace.

Third, I have worked to create a playful tone at times. This grows partly out of my desire to be vulnerable and personal. To hide this side of me somehow seems false or pretentious in a book of this sort. I understand that not everyone will appreciate these efforts. I have often witnessed a certain roll of the eyes and not-so-subtle shaking of the head on the part of my children and my colleagues, so I understand that my humor has certain limits. My wife, on the other hand, visibly adores everything I say and smiles admiringly at all my clever wordplays. I am grateful for this, of course. I trust the reader will find a happy balance, responding with a measure of discernment as well as grace. More importantly, however, my attempts at playfulness grow out of my conviction that most of us take ourselves too seriously. If we can never smile at ourselves, meaningful conversation among people of differences will be difficult. This is more of a problem than many of us admit.

Fourth, I have tried to be candid. I do not desire to participate in word games. I do not want to mask what I really mean. I do not want the reader to wonder what lies behind anything I have said. I appreciate the place of diplomacy in social interaction. I understand what it means to be wise. I recognize that sometimes the most appropriate response is to disengage from an unhealthy dialogue or relationship. But anything less than candid speech concerning disputable matters would be detrimental to the cause of unity. This commitment is difficult for many reasons, primarily because each individual has a unique world of meaning. Especially in highly polarized environments, words mean different things to different people in different contexts. I have learned to be careful. Communication is difficult in the best of circumstances. And when motives are impugned, clear speech is virtually impossible. Nevertheless, I have tried to write with candor as well as care.

Finally, I have done my best to be balanced. This is not a book about the divisive issues themselves but how we address them, how we treat one another when we disagree. My desire is not to pull for one side or the other. I want to speak in a voice that will resonate with small rural churches as well as large suburban ones, with non-American congregations as well as ones on U.S. soil, among predominantly ethnic-minority churches and those that are mostly white, with so-called progressives as well as those who hold to more traditional positions. In this regard I have tried not to take sides on any of the issues that divide our congregations except one. About this I will take sides: Christians ought to be able to discuss differences without rancor or judgment. Balance, in this case, is not a tepid unwillingness to discuss issues but a commitment to treat all positions fairly and to respond humbly.

The book's general structure moves from a discussion of our contemporary context to a consideration of several first-century churches whose problems parallel our own. I begin by putting a personal face on the issues that are fragmenting many churches, in the first chapter by focusing on several historical factors that still have considerable power over us and in the second chapter by addressing current behaviors and their effect on our children and our future. Over the subsequent four chapters, we will consider several churches in the New Testament that experienced significant conflict. Specifically we will look at Paul's correspondence with churches in Philippi, Ephesus, Rome, and Corinth. In each case these epistles will carry their readers, then and now, back to the cross, whose power alone can heal our wounds. In the final chapter, I will try to gather the threads of our discussion and suggest ways we can engage our differences in godly and constructive ways. The epilogue serves as a parable for the issues raised in the book, pointing the way to where the peace of Christ may be fully embraced.

Few would deny that things are not as they should be, that communication among Christians is not always constructive, that unhealthy talk undermines the mission of the church. The body of Christ indeed is broken. But it has always been broken. Our problems are not unique. In recognizing our brokenness, however, we find the courage to seek help, to come to the cross where we encounter the Son of God, himself wounded and broken. There Christ's blood was shed for the sake of sinful people. There Christ's body was broken on behalf of fragmented communities of faith. There, if our hearts are ready, we will find our way again.

CHAPTER ONE

HEIRING OUR DIFFERENCES

Facing our Past, Framing our Future

*The desire for truth makes reflective Christians
susceptible to a very widespread confusion in our
culture—the confusion of truth with certainty.*

—Daniel Taylor

I leaned back in my desk chair as the computer screen blinked on. I had a pretty good idea what was awaiting me in my inbox, and I faced it with a measure of dread. While the technological advances of recent years have been wonderful, they are surely both blessing and curse. Most of us love the instant access to information and the ease of electronic communication, but the tradeoff is a certain loss of control over our privacy, our schedules, and our lives.

I sympathize with the panic my mother experienced a couple of years ago in this regard. She and dad, both in their eighties, gamely worked with the little laptop we had provided them. On most days they were able to maneuver successfully through their handwritten directions so that they could retrieve email. But mom couldn't quite mask the anxiety in her voice when she called me one afternoon at my office. "I think I've done something terribly wrong," she said.

"What do you mean 'terribly wrong'?" I asked. Her voice trembled, "The computer says I performed an illegal operation."

I can remember the first time that message popped up on my computer screen a few years ago. I thought I was minding my own business, getting important work done on my office computer, but somehow I had broken the law. I feared the sound of sirens for a week. So I understood mom's distress. I assured her that despite the message on her screen, she, in fact, had done nothing illegal. "What should I do?" she asked. I told her, "Just close the window." There was a long pause on the other end of the line. I told her I would be right over.

During the past twenty years, computers have given me more joy and caused me more heartache than I could ever have imagined. I have found myself fantasizing sometimes about what I might do, say, with a computer and a hammer or, perhaps, a small nuclear device. But this particular morning, as my email program began to retrieve the previous night's collection of posts, my anxiety was not about illegal operations or unexpected program terminations. Nor did my unease relate to the assortment of unsolicited appeals that I knew awaited me, though I am sure there were folks out there who genuinely wanted to help me make millions of dollars working out of my home. Rather, if this day were like the day before, and the ones before that, I would have the opportunity to read a fistful of emails challenging my character and questioning my faith.

The first post I opened seemed particularly malicious. I didn't recognize the sender. As I scrolled down the page, I could hardly miss the fact that it had already been forwarded eight times. I counted over seventy addresses to whom it had been sent, six dozen or so individuals who had read the post then forwarded it to friends and family. I looked at each username but didn't know any of them. I stopped to think about the mental and spiritual processes that would have guided their behavior. I imagined them opening their inbox and reading the message for the first time. What course of reasoning did they follow? How did the person of Christ, who surely lived in their hearts, filter what they read? In what way might the Holy Spirit have been at work as they hit the "forward" button and started adding names from their address books? Did any of them question what they had read? Did they pause before hitting "send"? Did they pray? Did their consciences throb as they passed on the accusations without attempting to discover the veracity of the original post? Only after dozens of people had forwarded the message did anyone write to ask if it were true. No one seemed to question whether such means of attack were appropriate even if the accusations had been true. I sighed as I began to respond to each name.

Before playing the martyr, however, perhaps I should direct the questions differently. How did the person of Christ, who lives in my heart, affect my responses? In what ways did the Holy Spirit work in my life as I shared the story with others? What course of reasoning did I pursue when I said or thought unkind things? Did I pray? Did my conscience ache? Where were my compassion, patience, gentleness, self-control, and graciousness? When Christians disagree, how do we determine what is appropriate, what is helpful, what is right?

During much of my adult life, through years of preaching and teaching, in working with elders and church members as well as students and parents, and especially with ministers, I have become alarmed at behavior that seems uncivil at least and ungodly at worst. I cannot quite grasp it. People who go to church every week, who read the Bible, listen to sermons, take communion, and pray, people who say hello in the supermarket and root for their grandkids at soccer matches, who edge their lawns, drive under the speed limit, and show pictures of their new puppy at the hairdresser's, people of good will and good manners with high moral commitments and low tolerance for rude behavior nevertheless speak ill of others, spread gossip, criticize, disparage, and pass judgment on those with whom they disagree. And often they do so in the name of Christ.

For years I have tried to ignore such behavior. After all, who am I to say anything? Who am I to correct? Most people I know simply disregard criticisms. It is easier that way, and sometimes it is best. But often the inappropriate behavior cannot, or should not, be ignored. Elders cannot afford to turn their backs on gossip or divisiveness in their flock. When Christians sin against others, when lives are hurt

and reputations are sullied, the church has a responsibility to
address it. We are accountable to each other. Ignoring such behavior
not only compounds the immediate situation, it does long-range
damage to the church.

Over time, where would behavior of this sort lead? Whom would
it affect? If intolerance of differences and disrespect of persons
become pervasive, if they become institutionalized in churches and
universities, journals and lectureships, if they infiltrate what we
preach and inform what we write, then what kind of Christians
would be produced in the long run? What kinds of churches would
be created?

These are not idle questions. How we respond to people with
whom we disagree will not only affect our particular congregation,
but it will also have an impact on the larger Christian cause.
Moreover, how we treat one another and with what attitude and
tone will profoundly impact generations to come. It has always been
so, often in ways that we do not recognize in the moment. A look at
our past provides perspective on how we have become who we are
and casts light on the road we seem determined to take. A recent
event illustrates the point.

THE ROAD WE KEEP TAKING

In February 2004, leaders from the International Churches of
Christ and the "mainline" Churches of Christ met in a public conversation attended by a large crowd who listened with amazement
and even tears. On and off stage, apologies were offered and forgiveness extended. Men and women from each fellowship who had not
spoken to each other in years gathered in animated conversation and
penitent prayer. Families that had been divided since the early 1980s
awakened to the possibility of reconciliation. Individuals who had
caused or inherited the division were on this day people of peace.

Much had occurred over the previous twenty-five years.
Churches had split, friendships had dissolved, and angry words had
been spoken. In the late 1970s, a vibrant campus ministry movement
among Churches of Christ began to splinter. Divergent interests and
emphases spiraled into increasingly bitter rhetoric. Gossip became

common; hurtful things were said and done. Though I was a young man at the time, a graduate student, part-time campus minister, and insignificant player in the larger conversation, I experienced these tensions first hand and contributed, regrettably, to the unhealthy talk and toxic atmosphere. I witnessed, and in small ways participated in, decisions that helped create a deep rift. The fabric of the fellowship was torn in two.

The reasons for the split were complex. But no matter how substantial the issues or how heated the arguments, the division was not inevitable. Though many cannot imagine a different history, another story was possible all along. Every step of the way, choices were made that ultimately led to division. Of all the options available, the ones leading to unity were not chosen. They were, in fact, hardly considered. The motives of the individuals involved were pure, as far as I know, but the consequences of the decisions they and their followers made have been significant, perhaps irremediable.

Churches associated with the Stone-Campbell Restoration Movement in North America had been down this road many times. We knew the territory. We didn't need a map. As our spiritual ancestors had done in similar situations, we ignored those with whom we disagreed. We turned our backs and walked away. Whether as wide as an entire fellowship or as small as a dispute within an individual congregation, such division has happened before. Our history is littered with the debris of many separations.

In 2006, we mark the centennial of our first great schism. The scar of this division runs deep in our ecclesial psyches. We are rarely conscious of its power or its effect, especially since most members today know nothing about what happened or why, but it is a defining moment in our common history. It marked us and changed us, forming our various identities, how we think, how we worship, how we view God, how we approach scripture, and with whom we fellowship.

At the turn of the twentieth century, this movement was torn apart creating two major streams, then eventually three, along with many distinct tributaries. The presenting issues of the first division were instrumental music and missionary societies, but these masked other underlying causes including differences in how to interpret the Bible, disparate values among urban and rural churches, the personalities of influential preachers, and the impact of the American Civil War, whose long reach is felt even today. But whatever the precipitating factors that led to the controversies then, the division was not inevitable.

Several church leaders on both sides called for unity in the midst of the growing polarization. Individuals such as J. W. McGarvey and T. B. Larimore, however strong their opinions on the controversial issues of their day, refused to draw lines of fellowship over these issues. Some preachers implored churches to live in unity despite their differences, but this spirit did not prevail. We are heirs of that legacy.

Decisions made by people who lived a hundred years ago directly affect how we view things today, how we now act, what we believe and practice in our congregations. One has to wonder what it would be like today had other choices been made, had church leaders thought and acted differently. This great stream of believers who share a common commitment to immersion and weekly communion, to biblical preaching, vibrant worship, the authority of scripture, and the vital place of the church in the lives of believers, might have transformed the landscape of global Christianity had unity been a higher value. But a different path was chosen. In spite of growth over the past century, in spite of churches being established, missionaries sent, colleges and universities built, seminaries and training programs for ministers created, in spite of the ways God has blessed these churches, many opportunities were squandered. Today we are poorer for it.

In the a cappella churches of which I am a part, we have experienced divisions with numbing regularity. We have fought and divided over issues both profound and inane: pre-millennialism, pacifism, congregational cooperation, Bible classes, the use of multiple communion cups, the construction of kitchens and bathrooms in church buildings, the indwelling of the Holy Spirit, charismatic gifts, hermeneutics, women in public leadership, choruses and worship teams, cell groups, prayer partners, over/under discipling, and the nature of total commitment, among others.

Similarly, a separation occurred a half century ago between the Disciples of Christ and the Christian Churches, fellowships that share a common restoration heritage and from which a cappella Churches of Christ separated a century ago. In recent years, meaningful conversation between the two groups has been rare. The division is fresh, many of the feelings still raw.

Such is our inheritance. The question is, must it also be our future?

Discussing such issues in calm and civil ways is often difficult. Even though more than a hundred years have passed since the controversies erupted that initially divided us, many from the a cappella churches feel threatened when anyone wants to revisit those issues, challenge the defining narratives that were formed out of the division, or engage in meaningful dialogue with individuals from other branches of the Stone-Campbell heritage. Conversely, some from among the Disciples of Christ and Independent Christian Churches find the entire conversation tiring if not irrelevant. After all, they do not feel responsible for last century's schism. Similarly, my correspondence after the 2004 conversation between leaders of International Churches of Christ and mainline Churches of Christ indicates how alarmed some people are about any conversation in which past actions are reconsidered or critiqued.

For many reasons, discussing our differences is not easy. But several factors from our past have complicated these discussions. They are not the causes of our divisions, but they have contributed substantially to a climate in which meaningful dialogue about differences is difficult. I will mention three factors briefly before addressing a fourth in more detail, one that is more personal, more immediate, and closer to the root problem that has precipitated the climate of conflict.

The Fruit of Racism

First, constructive dialogue has been complicated because the racism institutionalized in the United States following the abolition of slavery and the Civil War, and continuing up to and beyond the Civil Rights movement a century later, has profoundly impacted the unity of believers within the movement. For Churches of Christ, this has meant almost a century of mostly segregated congregations. The legacy of racism, which even now many churches do not recognize or confess, has created a divided fellowship. African-American Churches of Christ have experienced a strong sense of brotherhood that is deep and precious but nevertheless is defined primarily by ethnic factors. Being marginalized or ignored by the predominant culture, in this case by white church leaders, produces over time a certain camaraderie and intensity of fellowship, to be sure, but it does not encourage healthy relationships within the kingdom of God. Such segregation remains the consequence of sinful behavior and must be addressed candidly.

Hispanic congregations deal with many of the same issues. While in many cases language differences create barriers, not every Hispanic church is Spanish-speaking, a surprise to many Anglos. Whatever their primary language, these churches could be embraced and encouraged by English-speaking congregations in ways few practice or even imagine. Ethnic and cultural prejudices among whites remain at play in the continued isolation felt by many Hispanic churches and leaders.

In small ways, churches are making progress in this regard. New and potentially healthy relationships have been forged across ethnic lines in recent years. Nonetheless, true unity remains illusive because of the pervasive effects of racism that continue to affect Churches of Christ.

International Churches of Christ, which formed their common identity well after the Civil Rights Movement in America, are more racially integrated than mainline Churches of Christ. Separate congregations formed around ethnic identities are unimaginable among these churches. Similarly, within the Disciples' wing of the movement, racial and ethnic diversity within congregations and among the leadership is common. Since the middle of the nineteenth century, in fact, such diversity has been a high priority among these churches. In contrast, several leaders among Independent Christian Churches have expressed a desire for greater ethnic diversity within that fellowship. In numerous ways, the unresolved issues growing out of America's racist past complicate discussions about disputable matters because talking about the implications of racism must take place at the same time that doctrinal issues are being addressed.

THE EFFECTS OF CULTURALISM

Second, meaningful dialogue between American and non-American church leaders around the world has been affected by culturalism, or ethnocentrism, which presumes that the manners and behaviors of a particular culture are superior to the others. This tendency has long been an American prerogative, however innocently and even benevolently it has been manifested. Whether culturalism shows up as a sort of benign paternalism or whether it appears in a more insidious form of colonialism, it always undermines constructive conversation because it rests on the basis of a presumed inequality of relationships. In recent years, this tendency has been challenged by the increasing inclination of non-American churches to speak, act, and worship in ways that reflect their indigenous cultures. This is not only an inevitable development, it is largely positive from a kingdom perspective.

In previous decades, many American-sponsored churches planted on foreign soil tended to exhibit American values and practices. This is not to disparage the churches and missionaries who began these efforts or to suggest that all of them exhibited the kind of culturalism described here. On the contrary, worldwide mission activity among restoration churches in the twentieth century is notable and praiseworthy. Courageous and godly men and women from the United States, working together with national leaders, contributed in substantial ways to the redemptive work of God around the world. However, as Westerners increasingly have had to admit attitudes of cultural superiority in relation to the rest of the world and as globalization has made every boundary porous and moderated the cultural hegemony of any single nation, so some American church leaders have had to reassess their views and feelings toward mission churches.

I have visited with national leaders on every continent who confess that they often talk one way when they are with Americans and another way when the Americans are gone. More than a few churches around the world modify their worship services out of deference to the visiting Americans who provide financial support. They do not know how to tell the Americans that they no longer desire to conform to American practices and styles. Also, many American Christians are not able to distinguish the gospel from their own culture. They do not understand that many of their congregational habits and styles are not so much Christian as American or, more narrowly, that they reflect a sub-region of the United States. Without this awareness, meaningful conversations about differences will be difficult at best.

A HERITAGE OF HISTORYLESSNESS

Third, productive dialogue within churches is complicated when some in the conversation manifest a certain historylessness, that is, a blindness to the fact that contemporary beliefs and practices have been shaped, at least in part, by the past. Restoration churches from the beginning were imbued with an impulse to skip over the past in an attempt to consider the first century alone. Most church members today reflect this inclination, either by denying that they have a history or simply by their ignorance of it. At its most insidious this historylessness takes the form of spiritual amnesia, a disease in this case consciously chosen by the sufferer.

Those who believe that their churches have been influenced by no one or nothing in the past, that people who just read the Bible and follow it will form a church that looks exactly like theirs, are not able to discuss differences of belief or practice constructively. Ironically, this deafness to the voices of the past taunts history to repeat itself, which has happened many times in the Restoration Movement.

To recognize that we came from somewhere, that our view of church, culture, the Bible, and God have been influenced by those who have gone before, does not give these individuals authority or power over us. On the contrary, our spiritual ancestors have their greatest power in our lives when we blindly believe that they have no power. Knowing that we have an intellectual and ecclesial history frees us from being bound by it. It helps us sort out what is of God and what is of our own making. Confessing that our churches have a past actually empowers us to do what the critics of historical consciousness most want: to be shaped less by other humans than by God himself.

Historylessness, however, does not function alone. Its partner is a sectarian spirit. If a lack of historical consciousness robs us of humility, sectarianism builds a fortress around us so that we cannot see or listen to others. It leaves us talking only among ourselves. Together, historylessness and sectarianism narrow our world, thus limiting the possibility of learning and growing. They make us smug. They create the illusion that no one else has anything to teach us. They undercut the possibility of relationships with anyone other than people like us.

Historylessness functions most destructively, however, by robbing us of perhaps our most important Christian quality: humility. If every other group is forged out of human labor and only ours comes directly from God, if all others are shaped by human doctrine but only ours follows scripture completely, then our only possible response is to stand over everyone else in judgment or pity. Without the humility that comes from an awareness of our humanness, meaningful dialogue with others is simply impossible.

Over the years, these factors—racism, culturalism, and historylessness—have frustrated our ability to talk to one another when we disagree. Each in its own way has limited our vision. Each makes constructive engagement with others difficult. More importantly, each of these obstacles has blinded us to our brokenness—our pride, our divisiveness, our sin.

One additional factor needs to be considered as we assess our past, one that has had a more immediate impact on our current climate, and one that lies close to the heart of the problem. As I reflect on my experiences growing up in Churches of Christ, this factor more than any other affected how I learned to view other believers. Over the years it shaped how many of us learned to treat people with whom we disagreed. A recent event at my congregation prompted my reflections on this powerful influence on my thoughts and behavior.

A Presence in My Home

I was sitting at one of the round tables near the back of the small Sunday School classroom eyeing the last bite of a doughnut that was resting casually on the napkin in front of me. I rotated in my hand the styrofoam cup that contained what was purported to be coffee but which tasted like finely brewed aluminum. My friend Donna began to speak. Members of our class had been invited to tell our stories—what it was like growing up in our homes, how we had come to know the Lord, what peculiar obstacles we had faced, who or what had inspired us.

Hearing these stories allowed us to understand each other better and enabled us to engage the weekly lessons with greater insight and compassion. I was not prepared, however, for the emotional impact of Donna's narrative. She described what it was like growing up in her home with Death as a permanent tenant.

Most of the time, Death is only an occasional guest in our homes, an unwelcome caller who seizes its victims abruptly or, perhaps, leads them away after a brief stay. Sometimes this visitor lingers weeks or even months, but it rarely takes up residence. But in Donna's home, Death had moved in and unpacked its bags. It was the unseen presence in every gathering, the taciturn participant in every conversation, the dreaded subject of too many nightmares.

Donna's younger sister, Martha, had been born with a rare blood disease. For Martha this meant no day without pain. It meant a life interrupted by emergency trips to the doctor, extended hospital stays, relentless tests, and agonizing medical interventions. For their mother, it meant her life was not her own. She was tethered to Martha's needs, wounded by her daughter's pain. For Donna, growing up meant seeing pain she could never ease, feeling guilt for her own occasional carefree moments, and witnessing the caprice of Death who only ground down her sister rather than taking her life and who ultimately stole her mother's life rather than leaving their home victimless.

All of us around the room sat riveted as Donna told her story of having to live most of her childhood days with this insistent visitor. If I were completely candid, I would confess that from time to time I leaned forward in my chair in order to peek at Martha who was sitting across the room with her husband. I was hoping to catch a glimpse of her reaction to the story her sister was telling, the story in which she also had lived—is, in fact, still living. I brushed the tears from my eyes with measured nonchalance.

As I reflected afterwards on Donna's story, I realized that I had also grown up with a powerful presence in my home. It was a somewhat vague, unnamed companion about whom I almost never spoke but who largely defined who I was and who touched almost everyone I knew. It was not Death. On the contrary, I do not remember fearing death at all or even thinking about it. Like most children, I went about my days as if I would live forever. Nor do I remember experiencing dread or the fear of pain. The presence of which I eventually became aware was of a different sort, but its influence was every bit as great.

My companion did not merely live in our home but also was a vibrant part of the life of our church, though I could hardly have distinguished home from church since one almost completely overlapped and defined the other. Its presence was not unique to our home. In fact, because of how my parents lived and what they taught their children, our experience with this presence was less substantial than that of most of my friends. But everyone I knew in Churches of Christ had a common experience with it. We didn't talk about it, but we felt it in every sermon and every class.

Its name was Certainty.

I didn't think much about other groups—"the denominations" as we always referred to them—but I was pretty sure they did not know Certainty the way we did. This companion was a great comfort, providing solace and reassurance to us all. It was largely what gave my peers and me such confidence.

Only in my adult life did I begin to encounter friends whose experience of Certainty in their home and church was painful or difficult. I can recall almost no negative experiences growing up in Churches of Christ. To this day, I struggle with those who feel bitterness in relation to this fellowship. I try to understand, but I cannot. I never felt the burden of legalism, though I recall classes and sermons on Christian duty. I do not recollect ever feeling repressed or judged, though I remember many lessons warning against the dangers of falling away and the horrors of hell. For me Christian living was not only full of joy, it was the only life I could imagine. Of course, being a Christian meant living the way we lived and believing what we believed, which is to say, being certain of what we knew.

I often had a difficult time understanding why others who read the Bible couldn't see what we saw. Were they just blind? Could they not understand what the scriptures so clearly taught? Or perhaps well-meaning ministers whose judgments were, nevertheless, erroneous, were misleading them. This, of course, was no excuse for following these false teachers, but it might explain why so few were able to see the truth. The only other explanation I could imagine was that they were just rebellious, doing what they wanted to do even in the face of scripture's clear teaching. Whatever the case, my people and I didn't suffer from such errors. We knew and practiced the truth. Of this we were certain.

The presence of Certainty was rarely talked about publicly. In fact, I remember as a teenager in the 1960s widespread concern that too few of us were sure about our salvation. When asked, "Do you believe you are going to heaven?" quite a large number, disturbingly, said they weren't sure. As a result, we heard many lessons about having confidence in our salvation. These were the first sermons I can recall about grace. But even then, we were certain that other groups were not part of the kingdom. We might not be so sure about our own salvation, but we were sure that others didn't have it.

I recall only a few sermons that said outright that we were the one and only church. Rather, such understanding was passed from one generation to another through a gradual, almost unconscious, absorption by continual exposure, like osmosis. I remember one time, though, in a sixth-grade Sunday School class, when we talked openly about being "the only church going to heaven." That is what we were, of course, but we were urged not to say this overtly to our denominational friends. That just wouldn't be considered polite. More importantly, it wouldn't be a good strategy for evangelism.

Certainty was present at every church service. It was a companion in every prayer, the unspoken assurance behind every sermon. I knew who was going to heaven and who was not. Those who were going to heaven came only from those of us who were "members of the church." Not all members of the church, of course, would go to heaven (who knew everyone's private thoughts and behaviors?), but clearly no one else would. There is a great deal of comfort growing up in a world where things are so clear. I just couldn't understand why those who were not members of the church didn't always like us or sometimes thought we were condescending. But that was just one of the consequences of living with Certainty. It was our burden to bear, and we bore it with purpose and determination.

Not everyone who grew up in Churches of Christ in the fifties and sixties experienced what I did. Some encountered the darker side of Certainty. Some of my friends recall being forbidden to serve communion because their hair was too long. I have talked to preachers who were placed on "heretics lists" in then-powerful brotherhood journals. I was aware of the down side of Certainty. I just didn't experience it myself.

I also now know that some did not grow up in a church where Certainty had a regular presence. These individuals recall an openness to discuss issues, public occasions of disagreement without division, and even events in which people from other groups were invited for conversation. But these churches were rare and were considered by many to be aberrations.

I admit that my perception of church as I experienced it in the middle part of the twentieth century is skewed. They are my memories, and memory is flawed. I am sure there was diversity I never saw and nuances of faith and doctrine I never perceived. Obviously, my description of church in these years is something of a caricature, but it is not a caricature that comes from cynicism or derision. I do not feel critical or even sad about those years. I became a Christian during those years. I love this church, and I find myself very defensive of her.

Throughout my childhood and adolescence, devout men and women nurtured my faith to full adulthood. My godly father taught me grace from the earliest days of my life. During my early teen years, he completed his master's degree in Bible for three reasons: so that he would be a better Christian, so that he would make a good elder, and so that he could have informed conversations about the Bible and church with his boys. My mother lived a life of devotion and service in the presence of her children. Even today, in her eighties, she spends a day a week at her congregation's clothes pantry and community outreach center. I witnessed people making extraordinary sacrifices for the gospel, saw missionaries live for decades in difficult surroundings in order to preach the Good News, observed countless acts of selfless service, received the hospitality and graciousness of hundreds of homes, and heard staggeringly powerful sermons from giants in the faith.

Moreover, I still believe most of what I was taught. I am more committed than ever to baptism by immersion for forgiveness of sins, weekly communion, the leadership of elders, freedom from denominational hierarchy, and the authority of scripture. My understanding is deeper now. I believe my perspectives are broader and my approach to scripture healthier. But the essence of what I was taught I have not rejected. The greatest problem was not what I was taught but the unexamined and ubiquitous presence of Certainty.

I do not mean to imply, of course, that there are no certainties, no absolutes. There are. The problem is not that we acknowledge the certainty of God at the center of things. It is in assuming that we have mastered these certainties rather than being mastered by them, that our understanding is the understanding, that our knowledge is complete while the knowledge of others is partial or flawed. The issue is not whether the object of our knowing is certain. It is. Rather, my concern is whether our knowing of it is flawless. It is not.

From the earliest days I can remember, Certainty made me smug. It enticed me into the sin of pride. It kept me away from conversations with those who might challenge me. But when those conversations came anyway, Certainty reminded me that I was right after all and that nothing the other person might say could remove me from my special place at Jesus' side. From Certainty I learned to smile knowingly at the fallacies of others, to dissect and destroy their logic, and to disparage their faith as well as their sincerity.

While Certainty, at least on the surface, served us well enough in the past—keeping our fellowship together, energizing our zeal for evangelism, inspiring our preaching—it is proving false in our current context. As the continental shelves of opposing cultures slide and crash into each other, as the ground beneath us shakes, and the structures we have long trusted begin to tremble, Certainty seems to have abandoned us. We have clear answers to many questions that our children and our culture are no longer asking. A growing number suspect the Bible was not asking some of those questions either. Our isolation from others is now our bane. Because of it, because of Certainty's betrayal, the very identity of the church as we have known it is crumbling. If we are not who we were, if what we knew to be true can now be challenged, if we can engage in meaningful and constructive conversations with others who are different from us and even learn from them, then who are we? If Certainty was the engine of our movement, if our exclusive claim to salvation was the justification for our existence, and if these values are collapsing, then what is our reason to exist now?

I ask these questions not to challenge the viability of the impulse toward restoration or the fellowship that has nurtured me so profoundly. On the contrary, I believe that this movement, with its passion for the Word and heart for the world, with its deep roots as a radical free church and its impulses toward countercultural values and behavior, is poised for great days. The question is, can we traverse these difficult times without hurting ourselves first? Can we talk to one another with enough patience and grace to arrive together at a healthier place? To get there we will need to understand something of our current social context, and we will need to address the self-destructive behavior that undermines our relationship with God and each other. In so doing, we will serve the spiritual interests not just of ourselves but also of our children.

CHAPTER TWO

SUFFER THE CHILDREN

The Consequences of Divisive Behavior

[When I was a child,] when people did not do what I wanted...
I would become angry with my elders for not being subservient
to me, and with responsible people for not acting as though
they were my slaves; and I would avenge myself on them by
bursting into tears. This, I have learned, is what babies are
like, so far as I have been able to observe them.

—Augustine, *Confessions*

My son was the one who ultimately made the choice. Jay was eleven. We were walking through the aisles of our neighborhood video store looking for a movie we both might enjoy. This is no easy task, as any parent knows. At his suggestion that we take home the latest Jackie Chan film, I simply put my foot down. There are certain artistic values I refuse to compromise, and Jackie Chan, no matter how highly acclaimed his acting skills, was not on my list of tolerability.

I began browsing the next aisle. There in the section of new releases, a British film caught my eye. It promised to be cultured, nuanced, and highly literate, with extensive character development and no bothersome chase scenes, violence, or nudity—just the sort of film to expand the budding mind of a pre-teen. I had not, until that moment, seen a look of sheer disdain on such a young face.

As a compromise he suggested we watch "Twister." This was no Oscar-winning movie, I knew, but the premise was intriguing and the actors decent. Helen Hunt stars as a tornado tracker, a storm-chasing scientist trying to better understand how tornados worked. However, she is overly curious, for my money, taking too many risks for her, or my, comfort. Sure enough, in the climactic scene, as the killer tornado chases her and her former boyfriend across a farm, with pieces of the barn and other pesky debris swirling around their heads, including combine harvesters and eighteen-wheelers, they jump into a shed and tie themselves by their belts to a convenient well pipe in order to ride out the storm.

As the tornado hovers above them, intent upon their destruction, they are vacuumed straight up into the vortex, only their belts and the solid hardware of the pipe keeping them from being ingested into the bowels of the beast. But the look on Helen Hunt's face is that of utter pleasure. She is one with the tornado, at peace with herself and the world, a smile on her lips and joy in her heart.

I thought of that scene recently as a fourth hurricane tore through Florida in a matter of days. In each situation, brave news reporters rushed to the target areas, gravely shouting above the winds how dangerous the situation was and why everyone should get out. Vehicles overloaded with photo albums, family heirlooms, furniture, pets, and, if room, children, were backed up for miles on the interstate as the evacuation progressed. But someone always remained behind, a cheerfully unconcerned soul confidently securing his mobile home against the winds or defiantly facing the approaching tempest while hugging a nearby lamppost.

Some people seem to enjoy danger. They thrive on risk and perhaps even seek it. I don't know if they are born with these inclinations or if these are nurtured through their life experiences. Most of us live more carefully. We are not anxious to defy gales or chase tornados. However, not all crises can be avoided or difficulties evaded, no matter how careful we are. To live is to experience adversity. We may not always meet our hardships with joy, but meet them we will.

IN THE NEW CENTURY

The church has always faced hardship. Adversity is our steadfast companion whether we seek it or not. Churches that are not equipped to deal with adversity are not equipped to be a church. To be God's people is to know what it means to clean up the messes that storms have left behind. It means experiencing grief and loss, alienation and suffering. To be the church is to know great joy, to be sure, but it is also to know heartache. At their best, Christians surround and support those who are in pain, who have experienced death, illness, divorce, and loss. They choose to enter the world, not withdraw from it, so that they might bear the pain of others, caring for the powerless and the marginalized, the hopeless and the lost. Christians share Christ's pain, exhibit his compassion, extend his mercy, and experience his rejection. It has always been this way.

I have known a few Christians, however, who relish conflict, who almost seek the suffering. Like storm chasers scrutinizing the radar so they might anticipate where a tornado will materialize, like those who sit defiantly on the front porch of their home as a hurricane approaches, some Christians seem to seek adversity.

I sat by a man on an airplane recently who talked so loudly about his church activities, who was so boorish about his Christian beliefs, I found myself recoiling. I kept nodding in a friendly sort of way as he regaled folks from first class to the rear galley with stories of his exploits for Christ as well as his views on God's will for Israel, Iraq, and the entire Middle East. He laid out for me his ironclad proof that the rapture was near, detailing recent events in Jerusalem, Baghdad, and Washington. He meant well, I'm sure, and he must have thought I was not very committed to the cause even though I had identified myself earlier as a minister. I kept trying to bury my head in a book, but I could never escape. He seemed to take pleasure in the contemptuous glances he received from the other passengers as he strode confidently down the jet bridge.

Most of us know instinctively that this is not what Christ meant. To suffer from self-inflicted wounds carries no particular reward. Being a disciple, rather, brings with it a natural estrangement from the world. We live by values at odds with secular culture. We should not be surprised that some find us strange. Suffering is an expected outcome of our commitment.

There is a pain, however, that is not natural to the church as God established it, that is not part of God's plan: Christ never desired that his disciples inflict pain on one another. It is one thing to suffer estrangement from the world. It is another to suffer it at the hands of our Christian brothers and sisters. Yet the history of the church is punctuated by personal attacks and internecine quarrels, by letters and sermons whose purpose was to denigrate and destroy, and even by bloodshed as ecclesial conflicts erupted into the political battles that dominate the histories of most Western nations. In our own ostensibly more civilized day, Christians still wound Christians. They criticize and judge, they malign and vilify. At least some of it, as in ages past, is done in the name of Christ.

To be a Christian is to live with adversity, whether it comes from life circumstances or at the hands of others, whether it leads to righteousness or results in less noble behavior. But our normal human encounters and the pain we have learned to expect as Christians become especially challenging during times of significant cultural stress. We live in such times.

We are facing a momentous social upheaval in the dawning years of the third millennium, and the adversity it is causing can scarcely be underestimated. We are caught in a cultural storm that most of us did not seek and do not desire. The peace of earlier days is broken; the harmony of what was, for many, a gentler time is undone. This storm cannot be skirted. Willingly or unwillingly, we will have to face it. Debris is already flying around our heads as we look for a safe place to hitch our belts. American school children search the web in order to see images of yesterday's beheadings, teenage girls wearing the latest fashion in bombwear walk into Jerusalem department stores, planes fly into buildings, walls are built, wars fought, ancient wounds reopened, ancient grievances redressed.

We are living through a clash less of armies than ideals, less of countries than cultures. These are not just the latest wars in a civilization marked by perpetual bloodshed. Something else is going on, something deeper, less clear, and less certain. A few souls seem to thrive in situations such as these, relishing the risks, face in the wind, racing toward the unknown, but the rest of us engage these times with a measure of anxiety if not fear.

No one can travel very far today without being aware that the world has changed, perhaps irrevocably. It is not merely the cultural clash between Islamic fundamentalism and the ideals and practices of traditionally Christian cultures that alarms us, though this development is disturbing enough. Even among Western nations, a fissure has appeared, a widening gap between the way people used to think and act and the emerging values and behaviors.

My present concern is not to address the substance of the cultural changes. These have been articulated and analyzed, perhaps over-analyzed, in other places.[1] Such changes include, but are certainly not limited to, the following:

- the critique of the philosophical assumptions and methods of the Enlightenment.
- the challenge to rationalism as the primary lens for interpreting and understanding the world.
- the rise of relativism and pluralism and the resulting hypertolerance toward most behaviors and values.
- the growing openness toward the spiritual and even the mystical.
- the blurring of traditional boundaries among some social groups.
- the consequent intensification of sectarianism that has developed among others.
- the decline of optimism and the presumption of cultural progress as prevailing social norms.
- the escalation of the effects of globalization not only on world economy and politics but also on local thinking and practices.

That the world has changed over the past few decades is difficult to deny. Whatever the causes, whether we have embraced or resisted these changes, most are aware that things are not what they used to be. What primarily concerns us here is the social unease this shift is creating and the attitudes and behaviors evident among us as we learn to live together in the new state of affairs.

STORMS, BATTLES AND DISEASES OF THE HEART

We can't escape the anxiety accompanying these changes merely by turning to our homes and churches. Not anymore. Evacuation to a safe place is impossible; wherever we go, the storms seem to find us. Estrangement and division, fragmentation and fear, have become the new norms, not the causes but merely the symptoms of the cataclysmic changes taking place everywhere. The social fabric is stretched and, in many places, torn. Only the naive and the reckless are not a little nervous.

One might hope that our churches, at least, would be sanctuaries, secure harbors in the storm. In many cases they are. Christians still rally around Christians, hospitality is practiced, service rendered, prayers offered, prisons visited, the naked clothed, the hungry fed, the Gospel proclaimed. In fact, I think there is considerable reason for hope.

I do not recall a time in my adult life when there was greater commitment to prayer, stronger devotion in worship, keener awareness of the needs of the poor and powerless, or more intense passion for global evangelism than what I have witnessed in recent years. Elders gather regularly across the country, sharing and encouraging one another and learning how to be better shepherds. More time is being spent in elders' meetings praying and pastoring and less time micro-managing and administrating. More and more preachers are returning to the hard work of textual exposition. Youth groups are demanding more time in the study of the Word and less time merely participating in recreational activities. Many North American churches are seeing themselves for the first time as mother churches for church plants rather than as dispensers of religious goods and services or as thick-walled fortresses against the encroaching pagan culture. It would be hard to encounter Christian university students from around the world, as I am blessed to do each year, and not have cause to hope. I witness their ardor for Christ, see how eager they are to serve, and know they represent hundreds of churches from across the United States as well as communities of faith from every continent. I find considerable reason for hope.

Churches are not just sanctuaries, however; they are also at the frontline. In them the culture wars are being played out. Many of them have become battlegrounds, arenas in which the conflict is being waged. While there is much to hope about, there is also considerable blood on the ground.

For healthy churches, this situation actually carries with it a measure of good news. In the same way that the immune system of a healthy person is often made stronger in its encounter with disease, so communities of faith often find strength in difficult circumstances. In such times, evidence of the Spirit is often discernible, spiritual illness identified and addressed, and antibodies produced so that the body of believers gets stronger. To change the metaphor, a forest is often replenished in the years after a fire because old brush is cleared away and new growth is encouraged. Thus it is with vibrant churches.

Many churches, though, are not in good enough condition to face the cultural changes we are experiencing. It's not that the fire is so great that the forest can't withstand it or the disease so virulent that the medicine can't treat it. The problem lies within us. While we are fighting many battles in the name of Christ, we often are doing so on our own terms and for our own reasons. In the language of the Apostle Paul, too many Christians today attack not the powers and principalities, not the cosmic powers of this present darkness, or the spiritual forces of evil in the heavenly places (Eph. 6:12). Rather, in the face of God's clear concern, they struggle against enemies of blood and flesh, in other words, against each other. There is great reason for hope when Christians are covered in blood, but not when the blood is their own.

In war, noncombatants are often those who are harmed the most, the unfortunate "collateral damage" of military objectives. Likewise, disease has its undeserving sufferers and a storm its innocent victims. On my desk is an issue of *Time* magazine containing an agonizing photo of a Russian mother in grief, hand against her scarfed head, open-mouthed in shock and pain, supported upright by two friends, holding in her hand a photograph of her little girl killed by Chechnyan terrorists at her school in Beslan. Some time ago my morning newspaper carried the picture of a young woman from Pensacola squatting in front of rubble that the day before had been her childhood home. Her face is stretched with grief, her mouth frozen in wordless anguish. Hurricane Ivan was merciless and indiscriminate in his assault. In the days before, it had ripped through Haiti destroying more than fifteen hundred lives. These tragedies seem almost pale in the face of the tsunami created by the earthquake just off Sumatra the day after Christmas 2004. Our minds can hardly grasp the pain of such a catastrophe. Perhaps 250,000 dead. Millions homeless. We see the pictures and our hearts are broken.

While the scope and nature of the damage is different, of course, many of us have experienced cultural battles and ecclesial floods that have wrought great pain to our churches and homes. I have seen the hurt in the eyes of parents and church leaders. I have seen the confusion and, at times, the anger. I have talked to Christians who don't know what has happened or what to do. I receive calls and emails from people who are looking for answers or trying to find out who is to blame. I wish I could tell them. I wish I knew.

Some of us find ourselves having been ravaged by these enormous cultural changes, like medieval villagers dazed in the aftermath of the Plague. This capricious disease has caused considerable suffering in many of our homes and left others untouched. Churches are at different places as this scourge passes through. Some were on the front edge of the epidemic during the sixties. The damage was done, the losses counted, the pieces have already been picked up and dealt with. Other churches have only now begun to experience the symptoms. In some cases, because they are afraid, they close their eyes and hope or pretend it will just go away. Others are making heroic efforts to respond. A few churches show little evidence of the outbreak at all. Some are confident and courageous, others are nostalgic or in denial. However Christians have responded, the pain that many are experiencing is real.

What is most disturbing is not that we are going through difficult times. Christians have always faced trials. The current anxiety within American churches of the Restoration Movement, for most people anyway, is not greater than the painful challenges of the early nineteenth century, or during the Civil War, or in the midst of the great division at the turn of the twentieth century. Christians through the ages have faced persecution, poverty, heresy, and debilitating sin among their leaders. Even now, churches in other parts of the world face challenges that few Americans can imagine.

Scripture is replete with descriptions of these sorts of trials. Paul provides a litany of his own suffering: "in danger from rivers, danger from bandits, danger from my own people, danger from Gentiles, danger in the city, danger in the wilderness, danger at sea, danger from false brothers" (2 Cor. 11:26). The author of Hebrews describes the torment experienced by many faithful women and men of old who "suffered mocking and flogging, and even chains and imprisonment; they were stoned to death, they were sawn in two, they were killed by the sword" (Heb. 11:36, 37). The book of Acts, from the arrest of John and James to the stoning of Stephen and the scattering of the churches to the arrest, trials, and imprisonment of Paul, describes the troublesome plight of the followers of the Way, a path followed not only in the early years of the church but throughout Christian history. In contrast, the troubles many of us are experiencing in the early years of the twenty-first century seem almost puny.

No, what is most disturbing is not that we are going through difficult times. What is most distressing is how we are responding to the current unrest, at a level of maturity that, in many cases, does not reflect grown-up faith. Sometimes, and not in good ways, I feel like a child again, surrounded by children.

LIKE LITTLE CHILDREN

I was twelve and my little brother was nine. All day long we had goaded, infuriated, pushed, and annoyed each other until finally Mom had had enough. I'm pretty sure it was Jim's fault. It usually was, as I recall, and my perspective on these matters is emphatically unbiased. The fact that he was younger than I did not remove his culpability in the sordid affair. After all, it wasn't my fault that he could put on such a smug face, and when he folded his arms and sighed in that oh-so-self-righteous way who could blame me for responding with a jab to his shoulder and a witty retort? I'm pretty sure that my clever tongue, along with a certain innocent smile, was among my more adorable childhood traits. For this reason, I suppose, I was somewhat taken aback that Mom seemed to be blaming us equally for this little scrap.

What surprised us both, however, was how she proposed we resolve the issue. I think she must have been distracted with supper preparations, or perhaps she was tired after a stressful day at work. I can think of no other explanation for her response that to this day seems out of character. She told us that she was fed up with our wrangling, that there would be no more fighting in the house, and that if we wanted to wrestle we could go downstairs to the basement and get out the wrestling mat. As she spun on her heels and walked briskly back into the kitchen, Jim and I grinned broadly and elbowed each other all the way to the basement.

Now, this was no ordinary basement. It was a little gymnasium, essentially an unfinished playroom adjacent to the main house, an ideal place for three boys to live and play (four if you counted Dad, which is only appropriate since he could beat us at any sport). We three boys spent hours down there every week shooting hoops, hitting tennis balls against the wall, climbing a rope, playing "shadow man" baseball, and generally expending our excess energy. My brother and I tumbled down the stairs, unrolled the mat, and lunged at one another with unadulterated glee.

My giddiness soured quickly. Jim apparently had acquired a level of skill and strength I had not noticed before. I began to suspect he had been preparing for this day, perhaps getting up in the middle of the night to lift weights and engage in some sort of speed training. Soon my scrawny chest began to hurt, and I was breathing too hard to wound him with a well-aimed quip. So I feigned injury and told him we would have to finish this little argument at a later time.

I was trudging up the stairs, towing my damaged ego behind me, when he softly called my name. I turned to face him, expecting perhaps an apology for all the many ways he had hurt me. I didn't even see the fist coming.

It never occurred to me to tell Mom what had happened. How could I admit to her, or anyone else for that matter, that my nine-year-old brother had beaten me up with one lucky blow to the face? I mumbled something about tripping on the stairs and spent the rest of the day in my room. Frankly, I didn't know that a lip could get as large as the one I saw in the mirror. Nor could I quite name the purplish hue I watched spreading across my cheek. I just knew that I would never argue with my brother again. I have kept that promise to this day.

Not all squabbles are so amusing, of course, assuming this story is humorous to anyone other than my brother. Certainly the actions that parents might wink at in children can become inappropriate or even repulsive if engaged in by adults. These are not the characteristics Jesus was emphasizing when he encouraged his disciples to become like little children. To be childlike is to recognize our powerlessness and then depend on Jesus. To be childish is to deny our powerlessness by disparaging others while serving and applauding ourselves.

Look at any sports event, Hollywood gala, or political rally. Childishness is the fashionable behavior of the day. It is not that we are surprised that grown-ups sometimes act like children. We've seen that before. Rather, it is how widespread it seems to be these days, and how acceptable.

Childish behavior among so-called grown-ups is so common we hardly notice anymore. Players strut. Movie stars preen. Politicians point fingers accusingly. Some corporate executives play "Look at Me" every bit as well as three-year-olds. One prominent CEO who lived the opulent lifestyle to excess was recently in the news. Shower curtains valued at $6,000 as well as a $15,000 antique umbrella stand adorned his home. He was accused of using several million dollars of corporate funds to throw a weekend party for his wife, the sumptuous feast crowned by an ice sculpture of Michelangelo's David serving as an indecorous dispenser of vodka. Most of us know kindergartners who would have exhibited more discipline and restraint. We live in a world of childish overindulgence and intemperance where moderation and self-control are often seen as signs of weakness. Like children, we seem to be interested in getting our way, or at least getting even.

Several years ago I witnessed a youth basketball game for ten- to twelve-year-olds in which the referees ended the game at halftime because the verbal encounter between the father of one child and the grandfather of another turned into a fistfight. The children, on the other hand, were mostly interested in getting their Kool-Aid. During that same season, the coach of one team threw a fit at the end of a game because he was frustrated at the two teenage officials who, he believed, had blown a call, costing his team the victory. He later apologized to the league for participating in behavior that embarrassed both himself and his players as well as humiliating the young referees. I know that story because I was that coach. Childish behavior is sometimes embarrassingly close to home.

Such conduct is not attractive in adults in any context, but when practiced by church leaders it is especially ugly and the consequences far-reaching. Some churches have seen their share of strutting and preening, though they often know it by other names. Not a few Christians have perfected the game of "Look at Me." And when it comes to combative behavior, some believers appear to have achieved a certain mastery. Children usually recover from fat lips caused by their siblings, but Christians are often indelibly scarred by the words and actions of their brothers and sisters. Gossip travels from hallway to home, from the office to the Internet, as people's names are sullied and reputations tarnished. The smug gracelessness and clever put-downs typified by secular talk radio shows and combative television interviewers have become common behaviors for some church leaders. In contrast, their victims often struggle to find their voice or a sympathetic ear.

Others use methods less vicious but equally wounding. They marginalize individuals who hold minority opinions, or they keep their congregations as homogenous as possible, minimizing differences and silencing dissenting voices. Too often, when individuals or families slip away, finding some other group, looking for someone who will listen to them and love them, or simply dropping out in discouragement, the church does not see. They come together to sing hymns, offer prayers, and meet at the Lord's Table to celebrate Christian community, and are unaware that some do not feel welcome or heard.

I would feel better, I suppose, if I could simply direct these concerns at others. There are plenty of folks against whom I could aim my frustrations, I am sure. But I am the offender here. I am the one who created the scene and shocked my young players as I publicly scolded the teenage officials. I am the one who has passed on gossip. I am the practitioner of clever put-downs. I have marginalized and pushed aside. And I have sung hymns, knelt for prayer, and received the bread and cup offered not only for my salvation but also for the whole church including people who are not like me or with whom I disagree, and I have done so with too little awareness of those whom I have injured or ignored. I am the sinner, not someone else. To quote that great twentieth-century philosopher, the eminent Pogo, "we have met the enemy and it is us."

What is especially difficult for me to contemplate is that these characteristics may be endemic to a whole group; they may be part of the DNA of an entire body. If that is the case, the prognosis could be grim. If there is hope for people like us—and I have staked my life on it—then we have some decisions to make. The significance of the issues and the urgency of our circumstances will not allow us to put off these decisions. The time is now. What and how we decide will affect our future and the future of the generations who follow.

BELIEF AND BEHAVIOR

We have to decide, first, what we believe, not merely what we have always believed, not simply what has been passed down to us from generations past, not only what we are comfortable with or what we want or what we like. This is not a time to clutch at church as we have always known it while avoiding conversations with people who think or do things differently. This will not work, not this time. Vibrant faith, instead, comes through arduous work, not work designed to secure salvation because that comes only from God, but the work of a servant or a student, the work of a disciple, of a genuine seeker. Such faith comes by asking hard questions and by challenging the quick answers. It blossoms in the rich soil between easy belief and utter unbelief.

Belief that thrives will not come to the arrogant or the self-righteous. It is more childlike in nature. Faith should not be identified with the smugness of Certainty. It is not the object of unreflective pride that comes from knowing that we are right, then trumpeting ourselves. Rather, it is a humble confidence that comes from knowing that God is right, then trusting him. Genuine faith, like the kingdom of God, belongs to the poor in spirit. Its beginning and end is God, not us. Faith, before it is a set of beliefs, is a posture of surrender

This also is a time to decide how we will act. For many of us, a great disconnect exists between what we believe and how we behave. This is true not only regarding personal morality but also, perhaps especially, our treatment of others. Some of us have assumed that the eternal ends we envision justify any means we employ, that we can speak unkindly about others if we think they are wrong, incompetent, or dangerous. When we see other people as misguided or foolish, their conclusions erroneous, when we see them as too traditional or too liberal, as unthinking or indifferent or naive, we feel justified in disparaging them. We believe it is acceptable to talk about them to others, to dismiss them or demonize them, to write them up or put them down. We can caricature them as "Pharisees" or "change agents" without having actually to deal with them as people, as creatures made by God and precious in his sight. We can set them aside or write them off without any attempt at meaningful dialogue or engagement in prayer.

But how we act is an expression of what we believe, a direct manifestation of our values and commitments. Our behavior is a window into our soul. If you want to know what I think about Jesus, then look at how I treat others. If you want to know my theology, then consider first my conduct.

What gives me the greatest concern for the church in these decisive days is that the behavior of some Christians reflects not the Christ of the Gospels but a vindictive and judgmental Jesus or a cynical and flippant Jesus. This is not what these individuals want or teach, of course, but their conduct reveals their theology, exposing a view of Jesus that is, at the same time, impotent and dangerous. Whatever one's positions may be regarding any of the issues that trouble our churches, such attitudes, reflecting both ends of the spectrum, are quenching the Spirit. The behaviors they spawn make the unity of Christ's church impossible. Moreover, these behaviors are driving our children away.

WHY OUR CHILDREN ARE LEAVING

Let me speak candidly to my own fellowship of believers. Is it surprising that more than a few from among the younger generations are giving up on the kind of church they grew up in? Is it completely unexpected that some of them, young men and women now in their twenties and thirties, are walking away from Churches of Christ? They are not giving up on Christ. They are not giving up on worship or service or discipleship. They are not giving up their conviction that church is important or that they can make a difference in the world. These are not like some in past generations who abandoned life in a church in order to seek God only through solitude. These young women and men love church and seek active roles in communities of faith. But many of them are giving up on the church of their childhood. Sometimes they do so in reaction to the polarizing behaviors of their parents and grandparents.

For many reasons, mostly related to the great cultural shift we are experiencing, younger Christians do not exhibit the kind of "brand loyalty" presumed in the past. In previous generations, to walk away from one's group was rarely considered. Those who did often had to deal with profound consequences, personally and in their families. But those days are gone. Young people, in general, have different values and make different choices. We can't assume that they will stay among us no matter what, that they will learn to live with the rules and practices of our congregations even if they don't agree with them, and that they will surrender themselves to fit the comfort and wishes of those of us who are older. They won't. They aren't.

This is an over-simplification, of course. Many, perhaps most, are not giving up on Churches of Christ, though the number of young men and women who are leaving is sufficiently numerous for the situation to be disquieting if not alarming. When they go to college, when they move to another city, when they get married, when they find their first job, at some point early in their adult life many of them simply find another church.

I recognize the risk in suggesting causes for this development. I am sure the reasons are far more complex than I know. My perceptions are anecdotal rather than based on surveys or interviews. But I do talk to many young people, and they reveal several common responses. I share them in the hope that they might be grounds for conversation rather than opportunities for judgment.

First, some young people are leaving Churches of Christ desiring to experience something profound in worship, something engaging and relevant: they want to encounter the presence of God. Some find this in our assemblies; some do not. Several have said to me that they do not feel they have worshipped simply because they have participated in certain acts and rituals determined decades ago by people they've never heard of. They are not likely to measure their worship externally, that is to say, by whether they merely have done the right things in the right ways for the right reasons. When they worship, they want to do so through means and in language that captures their minds and their hearts.

Younger Christians that I talk to are not impressed with accusations that they have been unduly influenced by contemporary entertainment. They do not conceive of their worship as entertainment at all. Moreover, they don't understand admonitions to play it safe. They can't conceive of worship as a particularly safe activity or the church as a place where Christians take safe stances. Many are willing to abandon the teachings of the church of their childhood in order to engage in something they believe is significant and alive, that is part of God's present working in the world.

We should be clear: when it comes to worship, twenty-somethings and their younger siblings are complex and diverse. Their passion for worship, for example, doesn't mean just "new" worship.

Many, in fact, are helping reclaim the value of more traditional worship, whether that means the American hymnody of the 1930s or the worship patterns and language of the early church fathers. They attempt to discriminate between what is good and what is not by criteria more complex than how recently the hymn was written. In my experience, the younger generations are not driven in their worship as much by music as many of us suspect. They are more focused on silence and prayer than the generations ahead of them. They don't just desire more prayers in church, but they model an intense, passionate, full-bodied, and openhearted life of prayer. Frankly, many aren't looking for church homes on the basis of what the congregations teach but what they practice—how they worship, serve, and love. When they do not see the Father adored, the love of Christ practiced, or the Holy Spirit welcomed in our churches, especially in our assemblies, they look elsewhere.

Second, many of these young men and women are tired of sectarian, legalistic church life and doctrines that confuse Gospel and opinion. They are not interested in churches whose leaders insist that all practices and beliefs are of equal importance before God, that erring in any area, including doctrines that can only be inferred by moderns who are steeped in certain notions of Western logic and Southern American culture, will cost persons their eternal salvation. They are not buying it any more. They don't buy the hermeneutic that produced it. They especially don't buy the attitudes that spawned it. Many are turning their backs on these kinds of churches.

We should be clear, however: the trends are mixed in this regard. Some younger Christians are weary of years of social unrest. In their lifetime they have known little else. They have been scarred by the divorce of their parents or their friends' parents. Many of their generation were aborted before they had a chance to be born. This generation has lived during days in which most cultural values have been challenged and virtually every lifestyle and behavior is viewed as a matter of choice. While sectarian churches have unintentionally pushed away many young people, they are also attracting others who, having grown tired of walking on shifting ground much of their lives, want a firmer place to stand. A church that sorts issues

into clear areas of black and white, led by confident and often
authoritarian leaders, and which still nurtures the presence of
Certainty can be attractive to some younger Christians.

This leads to a third reason, one that perhaps can be laid at the
feet of churches at the other end of the spectrum. Some are leaving
as the byproduct of an unwillingness by some church leaders to critique the beliefs and practices of other religious fellowships while, at
the same time, being critical of more traditional Churches of Christ.
Over the last several decades, many Christians have moved away
from the spirit, practices, hermeneutics, and attitudes of fundamen-
talist or traditionalist churches. But here is the irony: few people are as
judgmental as those who have left groups they believe are judgmental; few are more critical of critical people and intolerant of intolerance
than those who used to belong to such churches.

In their desire to be more open and in rejection of the odious sectarianism displayed in many churches, some progressive church
leaders find it difficult to oppose any practice or critique any group
except the more traditional churches in their own fellowship. In so
doing, they create an environment in which their children are unable
to make meaningful distinctions between what is central to the
Gospel and what is not, what is merely human tradition and what is
close to God's heart. In other words, if identity with a certain fellowship makes no particular difference, if the distinct beliefs and
practices of other groups are inconsequential, we should not be surprised if our children feel no compulsion about staying in our
churches. Thus many among the younger generations are not just
leaving because of closed minds; they are also leaving as a consequence of open ones.

Moreover, children who grow up in churches that pride themselves on being more open often tell me that they do not know how
to evangelize or what to evangelize about. It was clearer, of course,
in the age of Certainty. Those of us who were raised in those days
were given detailed instructions concerning how to teach others to
become "members of the church." But if sectarian zeal has been
removed as the primary fuel of evangelism, do churches even talk
about what should take its place? Do our children know the story at

the center? Many churches have worked so hard to keep their teenagers engaged, not wanting to make things overly demanding or boring, that they have emphasized too little the meaning of costly discipleship or the scandal of the cross. Too few children of the church know a sufficient "why" that would compel them to lead others to Christ. In the rejection by some churches of right wing rigidity and judgmentalism, they may have left their children rudderless in waters known to have swift and dangerous currents. They should not be surprised if their children choose to leave. They were, in fact, equipped to do so.

But there is a fourth reason many of our young people are leaving, one that confronts the very core of the gospel, and one that prompts the writing of this book. They see us arguing, they see us finger pointing, posing, and gossiping. They see us angry at one another, unable to discuss in godly ways issues about which we disagree, or they see us avoiding the difficult issues, preferring to talk about one another rather than with one another. They hear talk about the value, even the necessity, of dividing this fellowship, and they shake their heads. They hear the sermons and witness the attitudes of many whose self-appointed responsibility seems to be to label, name, and accuse. Or they witness individuals who are the objects of these accusations respond with disrespect or cynicism, deriding the poor fools who attack them so ignorantly. A generation is growing up that doesn't believe this is what church should be about. They believe they have other viable options, and many are taking them.

Often these issues appear quietly, at a congregational level. These young men and women are not aware of, or involved in, church debates. Rather, the conflicts appear more subtly and are therefore more deadly. People they admire in their church are muzzled. Elders become paralyzed over decisions, or they are overly influenced by a vocal few. Bible classes often don't discuss issues that matter. Fear pushes many deep into their fortresses; thick doors are slammed, keeping people not like them outside. Our young, informed by a different set of values, grow confused and discouraged.

One young man sat in my office after having stayed up the night before perusing a popular Christian online discussion board some friends had told him about. He began to read to me some of the comments. I quickly stopped him. Some of the posts were misinformed or silly. Others, however, were personal and cruel. "How could Christians talk about people this way," he asked. I had no answer. A group of ministry majors sat around the table in my office sharing their fears and concerns. One of their friends, a young part-time minister, had to endure a grilling from one congregational leader almost every week, not because of anything he was teaching or doing but because of where he was going to school. Is it worth it, some of them wondered, doing ministry in such a place? A young couple told me that they had moved to a community church down the street from where they used to worship. They said they did not want their little girl to grow up listening to their preacher publicly ridicule and condemn people with whom he disagreed.

We cannot afford to ignore these trends. We cannot justify apathy in the face of such concerns. Our silence signifies our consent. It is past time that we stop and address the divisive behaviors that many of our children will no longer tolerate.

Unity and Truth

My greatest concern, however, lies deeper than the fact that some of our young people are leaving Churches of Christ, as troubling as this may be. My greatest concern for all of us is that our failure to talk to one another when we disagree is a sin against God himself. When we are willing to jettison God's concerns about the unity of his church in order to defend the positions we hold, we blatantly transgress against God, against his heart and his will. This is more than a feeling of regret about what is happening to our children. I do not want merely to diagnose an unfortunate sociological phenomenon. We are witnessing a wholesale abandonment of God's passion for peace, his desire that his children be united, reconciled not only to him but to each other.

We were taught, most of us in Churches of Christ, that defending right doctrine should be contrasted with a desire for unity. In more than a few churches, truth is pitted against unity, if unity is discussed at all. It would be great to have both, of course, but in the battle between unity and truth, truth almost always wins. Anything else would be considered compromise. We must not compromise truth in order to attain unity, we have said. In fact for some, unity implies that everyone must agree about everything. But in reality, the issue is more complex.

We sometimes do not grasp that unity is inherent to truth, that godly accord must not be seen in contrast to good teaching but lies at its heart. Sound doctrine feeds unity; unity is essential to sound doctrine. When Christians are unable to talk to one another, are unwilling to listen, and cannot approach one another in gentleness and humility, when disagreement is marked by anger and accusation, when the church is the place where dissenting voices are muffled and opinions are squelched, when the unity of believers is not loved and sought, we are in those very actions embracing false doctrine; we are breaking the commandments and breaking God's heart.

Pursuing peace is not an optional matter for Christians. Not only do the times demand it and our children need it, the gospel compels it. Peace is not a divine afterthought unrelated to central matters of faith and discipleship. Unity is not a marginal doctrine that becomes a luxury for Christians whose primary concerns are elsewhere. Peace is what the cross has wrought. People formed by the cross become peacemakers. Those who are healed become healers. Those who are reconciled become ministers of reconciliation. That is what the cross does. That is the kind of people the cross creates.

Living in unity is not the byproduct of the resolution of our differences. To wait until we all agree before we engage in matters that produce peace is nonsensical. Unity is only possible in the midst of differences; otherwise it is not unity. Waiting to have unity until everyone agrees is like having cancer but refusing treatment until the malignancy is gone. Unity is vital to those who disagree. It mediates life and health in the face of staggering spiritual disease. Peace is not what we accomplish, it is what we receive, what we inherit. Peace is God's work, God's gift. Extending the peace of Christ is second nature to God's children, instinctive to godly behavior. People of the cross see the wounds of others and seek to heal them. They see divisions and seek to overcome them.

But the peace of Christ is not merely a gift to Christians, it is Christ's witness to the world. Christians take seriously Jesus' prayer for oneness. The unity of his disciples, of all those who put their faith in him, was on Jesus' heart in the last hours before his arrest. But to what end? For what purpose? Jesus is clear. He prays to his Father, "The glory that you have given me I have given them, so that they may be one, as we are one, I in them and you in me, that they may become completely one, so that the world may know that you have sent me and have loved them even as you have loved me" (John 17:22, 23).

The world will see Christ because his disciples live with one another in peace. Conversely, when Christians cannot be at peace with one another, the world's vision of Christ is obscured or distorted. Pursuing peace is not an indulgence for Christians; it is a matter of urgency.

Several years ago, while I was in graduate school, my wife, Jeanene, brought to church one of our neighbors, the wife of a student who lived in our mobile home park. Jan was a fellow Texan, so the two women were naturally drawn to each other. Jeanene and I had teaching responsibilities that Wednesday night, so Jan went to the auditorium. Class was taught that night by one of our most progressive members. I will call him George. He was a dear man, kind in spirit, warm and hospitable, but he didn't mind occasionally challenging people or disagreeing with them. These were the early days of the so-called "political correctness" movement in America. I was somewhat taken aback, for example, when I first heard George pray, "Our Dear Heavenly Parent."

Also in the class that night was James. He was our most traditional member. In fact, he told me on one occasion that he felt fairly comfortable with the label "legalist." On every issue, his concern was that we play it safe. He had a good sense of what the Bible said on most issues. He was a dear man, kind in spirit, warm and hospitable. These two men were among our most precious friends. They were deacons in the church and friends to each other.

Much of the class that night was spent discussing the "mortal sin" mentioned in 1 John 5:16. Not surprisingly, George and James dominated the discussion. They had quite different positions about whether we could even know what this mortal sin was. They argued strongly and loudly.

We had caught wind of how things had gone, so when we all got in the car, we were apprehensive. On the way home, Jeanene asked Jan, "So how did it go tonight?"

"It was great," she said.

This was unexpected. "Great? What did you think was great?"

"Well, these two men debated much of the time. I don't have any idea what they were talking about. But I could tell how much they loved each other."

That's what was so great. She noticed that they loved each other. She saw that these two men could disagree, even disagree strongly, these individuals whose worlds hardly overlapped at all, who found little ground for agreement on any issue, that these men deeply loved each other. George and James were both deacons, both taught Bible classes, both led in worship, both loved their wives and families, both exhibited a spirit of hospitality, and both exuded the radiance of Christ. When they disagreed publicly, even an outsider could tell how much they loved each other. Would it surprise the reader that Jan was soon baptized?

By this everyone will know that you are my disciples, if you have love for one another.

NOTE

1. For a brief description see Jeff Childers, Doug Foster, and Jack Reese, *The Crux of the Matter: Crisis, Tradition, and the Future of Churches of Christ* (Abilene: ACU Press, 2001), especially chapter 2. For a basic overview of the philosophical issues, see, among others, Stanley J. Grenz, *A Primer on Postmodernism* (Grand Rapids: Eerdmans, 1996).

CHAPTER THREE

PEACE AND PROXIMITY

Seeing in One Another the Glory of Chist

> *The Kingdom is to be in the midst of your enemies. He who*
> *will not suffer this does not want to be of the Kingdom of Christ.*
>
> —Martin Luther

> *Christian community is not an ideal which we must*
> *realize; it is rather a reality created by God in Christ*
> *in which we may participate.*
>
> —Dietrich Bonhoeffer

After several international trips over the last few years, I have had to make some decisions regarding food. I thought I could eat almost anything, but I have a clearer sense now of my gustatory boundaries. Freshly grilled silk worms are on the outside. Squid is on the inside, though sautéed pencil erasers have approximately the same texture and taste as squid when chewed. West African fufu is on the outside, Mexican menudo on the inside, monkey brains on the outside, kidney pie on the inside. Durian is way on the outside. For those who have never tried this popular Southeast Asian fruit, it looks like an overgrown cantaloupe covered with menacing spikes, and it tastes like egg custard that has been left to thicken for several days in a trash dumpster then eaten while sitting inside a men's locker room. Rambutan, on the other hand, though it looks to me like a large hairy grape, is one of the most delectable fruits I have ever tasted. I enjoy a wide variety of meats, but I have not yet learned to eat any of the canine variety, even if considered a delicacy in some cultures. I just can't get past the plaintive eyes of all the sweet little puppies we have had in our home, though after a few months with our first dog, Casey, I must admit I was sorely tempted.

We have all been in situations where we encounter practices or beliefs that are outside our comfort zone, most with more serious ramifications than what food we eat. Some behaviors, while considered normal and right to someone else, are beyond our imagination. We can't imagine how a person could vote for a particular candidate or hold a certain political opinion. We can't picture why someone would want to live in this city or that country. We can hardly fathom how elders of another church could possibly think a certain practice is right or good. Some things lie on the outside of our boundaries of imagination or acceptability.

THE TYRANNY OF THE PROXIMATE

You are probably familiar with Charles Hummel's often-quoted phrase, the tyranny of the urgent.[1] He suggests that people often are hindered from doing what they believe are truly important things because they are handcuffed by matters of unrelenting urgency. In such circumstances, they can't see or do what is most needed because they have been blinded or sidetracked by what is most urgent. Similarly, I believe most of us have a tendency toward a phenomenon that I shall call the tyranny of the proximate.[2] We often cannot see larger realities in the world because our eyes are so focused on what is proximate to us, that is, what is near, both spatially and temporally.

We tend to view everyone and everything through the immediacy of our own experiences. As a result, we sometimes find other behaviors, customs, and points of view strange or even wrong. This phenomenon is more insidious, in some ways, than ethnocentrism, which assumes that our own culture is superior to others. In contrast, those affected by the tyranny of the proximate are largely unaware of other cultures and cannot imagine other norms or, viewed temporally, that other times might produce different behaviors or values. When we assume that what is normal for us is normal for everyone, we are tyrannized by the proximate.

My two sons-in-law have seen this phenomenon first hand, often with a measure of amusement. Jonathan grew up in Brazil, Mark in upstate New York. Many Texans consider both places foreign, even exotic. Moving to Abilene to attend college caused them to rub shoulders with some folks who had never crossed the Red River or, if they had, were certainly showing no hints of it in their speech or behavior. They can hardly contain their mirth when they watch the drawl-laden television commercials of a local mattress maven or witness someone trying to communicate to an international student by speaking English very, very loudly. I could not help being aware of Jonathan's unease some time ago as he accompanied several Texans through the streets of a Brazilian city. We were noisy, laughing and telling jokes, teasing each other and making seemingly witty comments about local manners and dress, unaware of the social faux pas we were committing as every eye on the street turned toward us. When he gently suggested that we might tone it down some, we gladly responded by decreasing our volume from thirty to twenty-nine decibels and continuing on our way. Such behavior is not a problem in our world, so why would we imagine it might be in theirs?

As my family and I have visited churches around the world over the years, signs of the tyranny of the proximate have not been difficult to spot. In each case, Christians have a hard time seeing beyond the norms set by their own immediate history and experiences. The way things have been done in their location is extrapolated to the way things should be done everywhere. In one place, church members could hardly grasp that American women didn't wear scarves on their heads when they went to church. This is what all women do, isn't it? One minister said that he thinks large churches are sinful. "How can you Americans go to church and not even know the names of all the people you worship with?" he asked. We have talked to some Asian Christians who can hardly fathom why Americans don't kneel when they pray and European Christians who shudder at the ignorance of most Americans regarding the great but increasingly neglected hymnody of Western civilization.

Often the tyranny of the proximate works the other way as Americans transport their own customs and practices to foreign soil. In some cases those who grow up in churches begun by devoted and well-meaning Americans have a hard time distinguishing what is gospel from what is American because the two were never differentiated. In a relatively innocuous example, few of the dozens of churches we have visited outside the U.S. sing indigenous hymns. Most use translated American hymns even though each country or culture has its own musical modes and history. I do not intend to criticize this phenomenon or rob these churches of what has become a wonderful part of their worship life. But it is also a symptom of the pervasiveness of the tyranny of the proximate, in this case determined by what is proximate to Americans.

More poignantly, several years ago we visited a church where we were told by the local minister, "This is the most conservative church in our country." I asked what he meant by that. He told me, "You will find this church to be exactly like churches in America." That's an interesting measure of conservatism. In fact, the style of the service was almost identical to that of many American churches, though I had not actually attended a church like that in the United States since the 1950s when the missionaries were first sent. Again, the practices themselves were perfectly fine though the leaders were largely unaware at the time that much of what they were doing was almost as American as it was Christian.

Closer to home, I have often chuckled at how the tyranny of the proximate among predominantly white churches has been experienced by my colleague Jerry Taylor, an African-American professor and a great preacher. He exhibits remarkable patience when he speaks to congregations that don't understand that the responsibility of the listener is not to sit passively but to engage in enthusiastic, vocal dialogue with the preacher. I tell him that when his white brothers and sisters utter a quiet "mmmmm" or lose their inhibitions completely by unleashing a tiny, timid "amen," he should translate this in his mind as a noisy shout. To change the more reserved habits in the cultural DNA of these churches would require serious mutation.

Even when we focus only on our own congregation, the tyranny of the proximate is often evident. Many conflicts within churches occur not because of serious doctrinal differences but because the views and experiences of some of the members do not allow them to imagine the beliefs and practices of others. We tend to see things from our own point of view, with our own interests at the center, with our own experiences as the norm. If others have a different starting place or ask different questions or prefer a different approach, we feel threatened or baffled.

This disorder is especially apparent among those who by life circumstance or historical accident are in positions of social power. These people are often blind to how others see and feel because they rarely have to adapt their views or behaviors to anyone else's. That is the special advantage of being at the center of the prevailing culture. It is also why those who find themselves there can be so blind to the adjustments everyone else has to make.

Caucasians in the United States, for example, are often unable to understand how difficult things can be among ethnic minorities, even in church, especially in church. They don't mean to be controlling or unaware, but their approach or style is the cultural default mode that just comes with being in the dominant group. It's like breathing; most don't even think about it. Similarly, men typically don't adapt to the feelings or perspectives of women because they don't have to. They are largely unaware of differences anyway. Women can and often do adjust their way of feeling and acting to that of men. Historically, and sadly, they almost always have. Thus the tyranny is passed wordlessly, even unconsciously, from parent to child. Older generations assume, or at least hope, that younger ones will grow up and see things more clearly, which is to say rightly. Middle class families have a hard time grasping the experiences of the poor. Married couples find it difficult to feel the pain of those who are divorced or widowed. City folks don't always know how to comprehend life and church as someone from a rural setting experiences them.

Seeing things from another's point of view is difficult, and it is compounded when these factors are stacked on top of each other. Speaking as a middle-aged, middle class, white, married, urban male, I have many blinders, and those blinders are difficult to remove. Besides, men don't have to make many adjustments to function effectively in their world; therefore, unfortunately, they usually don't.

Let's be clear. To one degree or another everyone is affected by this tyranny. As we assume that our own practices and points of view are the norm and are blind to the significant impact of our own experiences, we are tyrannized by the proximate. We can't imagine how others could be right or at least okay. We know what we are used to, and we tend to like what we have always done. Most of us do not take pleasure in being pushed outside our comfort zones, but we seek familiarity and wear it like a cozy sweater.

When we are exposed to the unfamiliar, however, we are forced to examine the structure, history, and meaning of our own proximate life and experiences. Seeing another situation in a distant place or in the distant past gives us the possibility of changing the lens through which we see our world, of being more aware, more humble, and less insistent on our own way. To that end, let me share the story of a church I have grown to love, a tight-knit group that appears to be on the verge of unraveling.

FRIENDS AND WARRIORS

I doubt you will have visited this church. It is not one of the large, thriving churches in North America. It is located in Europe, the product of a missionary who worked with the congregation a short time before he left to plant other European churches. From everything I know, this has been a healthy church from the beginning. Unlike many churches that lose their focus and energy after their founding preacher leaves, this church has grown and thrived, with leadership quickly emerging from within the congregation.

This church is not like some I know whose members seem to

think their primary task is to come to church to be served, where ministry is viewed as what professionals do. I have seen this often. Church members, if they don't like what is going on, look for someone to complain to. Like a child whose babysitter forgot to cut the crust off the sandwich bread, they holler, "I don't like it that way." If they don't like the song leader, if they think the sermon is too long, if they don't like the plans for the new church building, they scream, "I don't like it, I don't want it," and the church, like parents unwilling to discipline a spoiled child, is held hostage to their complaints. I know one man who for years withheld his giving to the regular contribution of the church because he didn't like several decisions made by the elders. He moved his contributions from one narrow cause to another only on the basis of whether he liked it. Nevertheless, the elders, who cared about his spiritual health, held their ground and refused to cut the crust off his bread.

In contrast, this European church doesn't seem to have many members who view themselves as mere attenders of worship services, hoping to get something good and giving only to what they like. Instead, they see themselves as partners with one another for the gospel's sake. They have experienced some opposition, but that is often the case in churches who see their primary work as living faithfully and ministering effectively in their specific situation rather than seeking the approval of others elsewhere. Still, these attacks have taken their toll. The members are noticeably anxious about it all.

The church is quite generous. Though they are far from being wealthy, they have given of their resources to other Christians in need, probably more than they could afford. Similarly, they have sent representatives of the church to serve others who were in very difficult situations. These individuals risked a great deal to engage in such missions, but they did so without complaint or expectation of reward. Much more can be said about this church, of course, but perhaps you get a sense as to why I love them and why I am drawn to them.

In spite of all they have accomplished, however, a shadow hangs over the church. The seeds of a conflict have begun to take root. Its ministries have helped numerous people, but this good work is being affected by growing tension within the church. I share with you what I know of their situation because if these things can happen to a healthy church like this, they are likely to happen to churches like yours and mine.

I don't know all the details. The specifics are probably unimportant. But clearly relationships are being affected. The trouble would probably make more sense if I were to tell you that it was taking place among the elders or within the ministry staff. That is usually the case, at least in my experience. I have had several recent long distance phone conversations with church leaders whose congregations are being torn apart because of friction among the leaders, one because of church finances, one because of mutual fear and distrust between the elders and the preacher, and one because of elders who have competing visions for their church. The consequences of these conflicts may be profound. But the issues within our European church are different. Though the troubles are not coming from the preacher or elders, the consequences are just as great, perhaps greater.

A disagreement has arisen between two people, two old warriors who have been part of the vision and life of the church almost from the beginning, two women whose work has been indispensable to its effectiveness. To indicate that the issues are merely between these two would be unfair, of course. When people can't get along, the whole church is affected. Apparently several are having a hard time seeing beyond themselves, unable to imagine how the others could think and act as they have.

I don't know for sure, but I can envision each of them coming to the place where they meet for worship. One, along with her supporters, sits on one side. The other, with her faction, sits across the way. Hymns are sung, scriptures read, and prayers offered, but they can't look at each other. The bread and cup are passed. Each woman wonders how the other could participate in good conscience. After all, they each know what the other has said, what the other has done. Both of them believe they are right. Each feels wounded. Neither will back down. Neither will compromise. Both have been tyrannized by what is proximate to them, their own interests and experiences, their own hopes and loves. They are unable, or unwilling, to see from the perspective of the other.

The missionary who planted the church is aware of what is happening, of course, and he is greatly concerned. He has had a long and good relationship with this church. These two women worked closely with him while he was there. They are his friends. Though he has moved on, he cares about this church and still has a measure of influence, so he wrote them a letter. I should tell you this is not a private letter; otherwise I would not have a copy and would feel it inappropriate to share it this way. He wrote a letter to the whole church. He intended it to be read publicly in the assembly. As far as I know, it was. I do not know its effect, not on them at least. On me it has been profound.

I'm going to quote from the letter as he makes his closing argument. Please forgive the references to people's names, but I know of no other way to make this crucial point. He says, "My dear brothers and sisters, whom I love and long for, my joy and crown, stand firm in the Lord....I urge Euodia and I urge Syntyche to be of the same mind in the Lord."

A Word to Y'all

You know this letter, of course. You have read it before. The writer is Paul. The European city is Philippi in Macedonia. These are not abstract holy words written so that we might place charming Christian sayings, fittingly framed and matted, on the walls and desks of our homes and offices, exhorting all who enter to rejoice in the Lord always. These words are not mere fodder for devotional thoughts or an imprint for the next t-shirt. All of these are innocent usages, I am sure, but they miss the point of the letter. I doubt Paul could ever have imagined that such a thing might happen twenty centuries later. Our task is to see this letter, as much as possible, as it was first received.

Especially because several verses in Philippians 4 are among the most familiar in all of Scripture, we must be careful to see why Paul wrote in the first place. He felt a great responsibility for this church. He was close to many of them, and he loved them deeply. This church was exemplary in its service and its concern for others. But that model of service and sacrifice was being undercut. A conflict between two of his friends and co-workers was in the making. If that happened, much that had been accomplished by the church in the name of the Lord would be threatened.

Paul writes them to say several things. First, he wants to express his gratitude. They have been very kind to him while he has been in custody. They sent Epaphroditus as an emissary from the church in order to serve Paul and bring him gifts. Epaphroditus almost lost his life carrying out his assignment. In fact, Paul's own life is in danger. He knows the church is anxious about all of this. He is grateful for their concern and their support for him as well as for their brother. He wants them to know that everything that has happened to him is for the benefit of the gospel, even his imprisonment. He is thankful for their partnership, of course, but he is concerned that they not miss the larger point about God's love and care. He wants them to know that even if they had not helped him, he would have been all right because he was in God's hands. If he had received no help, he would have been content. In fact, he says, he could be content if he had nothing just as he could if he had plenty (4:10-12). This is what he is referring to when he says he can do all things through Christ who gives him strength (4:13). Christ will empower him to face whatever he must face, to live with courage and contentment in any and all circumstances. To his dear friends in Philippi, he says thank you and do not worry. No matter what, he will be all right.

Second, Paul is concerned about some opponents who could potentially create problems in the church. He refers to them as dogs, as evildoers and mutilators of the flesh (3:2). In contrast to what Paul had been teaching, they are trying to establish their own righteousness through lawkeeping (3:9), but they may also be practicing a sort of libertarianism—"their god is their belly; their glory is in their shame" (3:19). Paul calls them enemies of the cross of Christ (3:18). Clearly this group has caused no small amount of anxiety in the church.

Third, Paul wants to address the problems that are escalating within the church. Some are acting selfishly, not seeking the best interests of others. Some are murmuring and arguing. And Euodia and Syntyche can't get along. Whether the tension has erupted into a full-fledged quarrel is unclear. The point is the same either way. Left unchecked, the disagreement could affect the mission of the church.

The key word in these early verses is "all," which is found repeatedly in the text. He offers his greeting, "Paul and Timothy, servants of Christ Jesus, to all the saints in Christ Jesus who are in Philippi, with the bishops and deacons." He pointedly sends greetings to all of them, not one group or the other but all of them: "Grace to you and peace from God our Father and the Lord Jesus Christ." We should not rush too quickly past this phrase, however common it may seem. Two words deserve a note. First, while Paul typically greets his respondents with a salutation of grace and peace, the word "peace" will carry special significance in this letter. Suffice it to say for the moment that peace is not merely a feeling of general well-being. Peace is primarily a relational word. To receive peace is to be in right relationship with God and others. It is to live in a spirit of reconciliation.

Second, he offers this blessing of grace and peace to "you." English doesn't help us much here. English speakers are often frustrated knowing how to distinguish the second person singular from the second person plural. That is to say, "you" can refer to one person or many, and the context is not always clear. As steeped in individualism as we are, our tendency is to read most occurrences of "you" in the New Testament as singular, so we make applications to our individual lives. Most of the time, however, the word is plural and the application meant for the church as community. Here Paul offers grace and peace to "you." To explain this better, I need to take a brief excursion into an important substratum of American culture, a digression I trust you will forgive.

I grew up in West Texas and became aware at a fairly young age that we spoke a regional dialect not shared by everyone in the nation. That became relatively clear when I was about five and tried to explain to someone on a family trip to California that my daddy, who owned and operated a number of gasoline stations in town, was in the "awl bidness," a profession they apparently don't have in Los Angeles.

Though outsiders often make this mistake, I should be absolutely clear that West Texas is not in the South. Most people who live up North can't distinguish between the accents of Savannah and Lawton, between Mobile and Midland. The dialects of the two regions are not the same, by accent or by vocabulary. One word, however, that Southerners and Westerners share is "y'all." This is a fine word, originated for noble purposes. Because the word "you" can be both singular and plural, the contraction "y'all" seems like a happy solution. It is easy to see how "you all" slurred into "y'all," in the same way, I suppose, as the English have come to call Worcestershire "Woorshtersure," much to the puzzlement of American condiment users everywhere.

The problem, from the standpoint of us Westerners, is that some Southerners wasted the advantage of this handy contraction by allowing "y'all" to become singular as well as plural. In Birmingham or Jackson, if people say "y'all come," they might be referring to just one person, though you can't be absolutely certain. You can surely see the advantage that was squandered in this unfortunate shift.

We Westerners don't have this problem, in the same way that we don't have the problem of pretending that grits is a breakfast food edible by humans. (And since I am not from the South, I don't know for sure whether grits is singular or whether they are plural, but that's another digression altogether.) Those of us who live in the Southwest normally employ "you" for the singular and "y'all" for the plural. Enterprising Southerners, however, in an attempt to address the confusion caused by the use of "y'all" in the singular, created a wonderful and uniquely Southern expression: "all y'all." When they look at you and say "y'all come," you don't know for sure, but they might mean just you. However, if they say "all y'all," then you can have confidence that everyone in your family and any-one else you know are invited.

As Paul writes to the Philippians, he addresses "all y'all." He consistently uses the second person plural. He extends grace and peace, he gives thanks, he provides words of exhortation to "all y'all." He prays, "I thank my God every time I remember you all." He prays for all of them knowing that God began a good work among them all. He knows that they all hold him in their heart, that all share in God's grace, and that he longs for them all with the compassion of Christ Jesus. His prayer is that "the love of all of you may overflow more and more with knowledge and full insight to help all of you determine what is best, so that in the day of Christ all of you may be pure and blameless, having produced the harvest of righteousness that comes through Jesus Christ for the glory and praise of God."

This inclusive language cascades through the letter. He loves them all. They are all dear. They are all children of God. They are all precious in God's sight, having shared in the gospel with Paul from the very earliest days. He communicates his affection for them all, and he prays that they all may learn to love each other, not blindly, but with full insight so that they might be able to see past their immediate circumstances and be able to determine what is best for the whole church.

He tells all of them how his own trying circumstances are actually advantageous for the gospel and to them. He admits that it would be personally advantageous if he died, but that he is content to remain in the flesh for a while longer because he can continue to partner with all of them and see their progress when he comes to visit them. He challenges all of them to live their lives as a credit to the Gospel. He calls them to be united, to stand together in one spirit, to work side by side with each other, to serve with one mind. He respects them all and offers these words of encouragement. As chapter 2 unfolds, however, his language begins to focus more specifically on the relational issues at hand.

Song of Sorrow, Song of Hope

Deep in the psyche of our family is an inclination to respond to almost every situation with a line from a song. All of our minds just run this way, I'm afraid. I'm not sure where this came from, for me at least. My parents when I was growing up were actually fairly normal people, so my urge to burst out with a refrain from the Beejees or Paul Revere and the Raiders, fine groups both, can be blamed only on me. Jeanene, on the other hand, comes by this trait more naturally. Her father often sang old Stamps-Baxter hymns in the family devotionals by attempting to vocalize all four parts at the same time. When the grandkids were around, he responded to their antics with lines, or sometimes entire stanzas, from songs he had wrestled out of country or folk music obscurity. Somehow our kids found his singing more amusing than that of their own parents. One sleepy daughter might announce to us, "I need to go lay down," at which point her parents, without hesitating a second, would respond in perfect harmony, "Lay your head upon my shoulder. Lay your warm..." but by then, after a dramatic roll of her eyes, she would already have left the room so she wouldn't have to endure the sheer humiliation of it all.

There is something about singing that affects people in profound ways. To this day, years after their grandpa's death, our children cannot sing "Jesus Is Coming Soon" without thinking of him. Songs stay with us. I think that is why, at least in part, Paul says to the Ephesians, don't spend your time getting drunk but be filled with the Spirit instead, singing songs, hymns, and spiritual songs among yourselves, singing and making melody to the Lord in your hearts (5:18, 19). When you need to respond to a difficult situation, don't let the songs that bubble up into your consciousness be from old drinking songs but rather from the spiritual songs that now fill your life.

That Paul's concerns about the impending Philippian crisis called to his mind a song, then, is not surprising. He quotes one that he and the Philippian church had likely sung together, a song employed to bury his message deep into their hearts: "Christ Jesus, though he was in the form of God, did not regard equality with God as something to be grasped." It was a fine song. Here is how Paul frames it, beginning in chapter 2.[3]

> I want to talk to all of you about how you should treat each other. But I am going to ask some questions first. The answers should be obvious. Have you gotten anything out of following Christ? Of course you have. Has love made any difference in your life? Does it mean anything to you that you have been in a community of the Spirit? Have you experienced any compassion or genuine care? Of course. Absolutely.

.

Then give me joy by learning how to agree with each other, by loving each other, by being in full relationship, and by focusing on things that matter.

Don't make any decision on the basis of what is best for you. This is not about you. Don't act only out of what you like or what you have experienced. Don't be limited by your inability to imagine how the other feels. Stop thinking of yourselves first. Rather, be humble and put yourselves in the shoes of others, seeing them as better than yourself. Look first at what blesses others rather than what pleases you.

I know you are not hearing this for the first time. Do you remember the song we used to sing in church?

> Jesus Christ being in form God
>   knew he was God's equal,
> but he did not fight to keep his place,
>   He set it aside,
>   becoming a slave,
>   being born a man.
> When he became human,
>   he became humble
>   and was obedient unto death,
>   death on a cross....

Do you understand? Do you get it? That's the mind I want you to have. That's how I want you to act. If Christ was willing to give up all the advantages he had as God's equal, if he didn't cling to his privileges when his father asked him to give them up in order to serve you, why do you seek advantage and position when he is asking you to step down and serve others? Christ did not seek what was best for himself. If he had done that, where would you be now? But he chose to become nothing; he allowed himself to be a slave. He became human. He humbled himself completely. He was obedient not only in dying but by allowing himself to be humiliated in a scandalous death. Does his sorrow give you any hope? Does his suffering affect how you live? Does his death change how you treat each other?

You seek exaltation by having the superior position, by winning, by getting your way. Can you see the difference? You seek to win; but as you do, you lose. Christ, on the other hand, did not seek to be on top at all. But as we have sung together, God exalted him and gave him the name that is above every name so that at the name of Jesus every knee should bend in heaven and on earth and under the earth and every tongue should confess that Jesus Christ is Lord to the glory of God the father.

Do you get it yet? Your task is to see things from the other persons' point of view. It is not to assume they will see things from yours. This is not about you getting your way—beating the other, being right. Your task is to make yourselves nothing, serving the others, being obedient to God no matter what. Your job is to serve; God's job is to exalt. You do your part. He will take care of his.

Christ's life modeled the point Paul is making. In looking at Christ's concern for others, which led to his death, Paul addresses directly what we earlier referred to as the tyranny of the proximate. Rather than beginning with their own interests, with what makes them comfortable, they should step outside of what they want and like and concern themselves with the needs and interests of others. They are to see things from the others' perspective, understanding their needs and desires, empathizing with their pain. The great hymn serves as Paul's foundation for everything else he will say in chapter 2. If you imitate Christ, you will serve others, and your petty disputes will seem insignificant.

Paul then charges his readers to imitate three others. First he tells them to follow his own example. He is willing to be sacrificed for their sakes, a bold statement that had implications about their own behavior toward each other. Then he presents the example of Timothy. All the others seem to be looking first to what is best for themselves. Timothy, in contrast, is more concerned about them.

Paul's sending of Timothy to Philippi serves as a pointed gesture about how they should behave toward each other. Finally, Paul calls them to consider one of their own members, Epaphroditus. They had sent him to minister to Paul's needs, and he had almost died on the mission. This model of self-giving comes from their own church. Paul is anxious to send him back to live and work among them.

Did they understand? Nothing they have is worth keeping if they lose Christ. A victory of some sort in a church quarrel means nothing. Could they back down even if they didn't think they were wrong? Could they live with the appearance that the other one was right? Could they swallow their pride for the sake of the church? What would they be willing to give up in order to know Christ truly and serve him fully?

The assembled church tries to absorb Paul's message as the reader of this letter reaches the halfway point. I doubt at this juncture, as they heard these words read for the first time, that the implications were fully apparent. We, of course, already know how the letter ends. We know the names of the two greatest offenders. We will have to let the full impact of the letter dawn gradually on the Philippian church as the public reading continues.

The Peace of God and the God of Peace

Can you imagine what the two women and their supporters were thinking as Paul's letter was read to the church? I don't know exactly when it hit them that this was not going to be a harmless mission report from their former preacher. Did they pick up the hints during Paul's opening greeting and prayer? Perhaps not. But my sense is that once the language of "same mind" and "same love" was spoken, when the reader said the words "selfish ambition," "conceit," and "not looking to your own interests," their palms began to sweat and their hearts began to race. I can sense the blood starting to rise in their cheeks. They are not looking at each other. They are looking at no one.

A few nervous coughs fill the room as the public reading of the letter continues. Paul is planning to send both Timothy and Epaphroditus to them. That's good news, but excitement about their impending visit doesn't mask the potential crisis facing the church, nor does it hide Paul's pointed admiration of the self-sacrifice of these two men in contrast to how some in the church are acting. Several folks shift in their seats.

As the reader arrives at the section where Paul tells them to "beware of the dogs," everyone sits at attention. This is strong language. Paul's defense of the church in the face of these opponents is encouraging. The two women try to catch their breath. Maybe the hard part is over. Maybe the point has been made.

The reader gets to the part where Paul considered every advantage he had as nothing, as rubbish. One might wonder if everyone in the church could say the same. As Paul speaks of what he gave up in order to know Christ, of his sharing in Christ's sufferings, of his pressing on to reach the goal of attaining the resurrection of the dead, they all are touched by his passion and eloquence. Several of them nod their heads. Euodia senses that the worst is over. She leans over and whispers something to the woman next to her, and they both manage faint smiles. Syntyche begins to pull at a lose thread in her garment. She makes a mental note to do some mending this week.

"Therefore my brothers and sisters," the reader continues—he is getting near the end now, "whom I love and long for, my joy and crown, stand firm in the Lord in this way, beloved." The reader pauses and looks at the room. No one makes a sound. "I urge." This is the first time these words have been uttered in the entire letter. Paul normally says this only once. It is a way of emphasizing a point. New Testament Greek has no bold print, no italics or exclamation points. Certain phrases were used to highlight what was especially important. "I urge...." Something close to the heart of Paul's letter would follow.

The reader speaks the words slowly and emphatically. "I urge Euodia and I urge Syntyche to be of the same mind in the Lord." You can feel the shock washing over the room. Euodia's mouth drops open. Syntyche's friend grabs her by the arm. The room is silent. He has called them by name.

Paul was not making a public spectacle of them. This was not an article in the religion section of the Philippi Times-Herald. He didn't post flyers on notice boards at the central market. He didn't write the churches at Corinth, Berea, and Thessalonica to make sure they included the names of these two women in their bulletins. This was a problem for the Philippian church to handle. Even as Paul's letters began to circulate later from church to church, eventually being gathered in what would become the collected documents of the New Testament, no one elsewhere assumed that they had responsibility for what happened at Philippi. Paul's intent was to help, not to embarrass or to shame, but he did so pointedly.

Divisive behavior is not to be taken lightly, and the church has responsibilities to deal with it. When churches are fractured, when people are unable to see past their own perspectives and interests, when friends are lined up and sides are taken, when gossip spreads and ministries diminish, the church must wake up. The message of the gospel is at stake. The fabric of the church is at risk.

Paul doesn't mince words. He calls these women by name, these precious friends of his, these fellow workers in the gospel. He never doubts their relationship with God. This is not about whether they are saved. They and the rest of his co-workers, including Clement, have their names recorded in the book of life. But if they continue in their present behavior, the church will be damaged.

Paul calls for his "loyal companion," an unnamed participant in this drama, to help these women. He or she knew to whom Paul was referring. Whether others in the church did is unclear. Paul urges this person to intervene on behalf of these women.

Ancient letters often end with general exhortations. Paul follows that practice here. But as he moves to the next few sentences, among the most familiar and beloved verses in all of scripture, he is not introducing a series of new topics, throwing in some random admonitions to round out the letter. Paul continues here the themes and issues he has already put on the table. After publicly calling for Euodia and Syntyche to stop their divisive behavior, he does not suddenly begin to ruminate on the subject of joy. We as modern readers must not lose our momentum. The tension between these two women and perhaps others in the church is beginning to create problems. The church's effectiveness as a community of believers is at stake. Paul addresses this directly:

Do not let these problems rob you of your essence as Christians. Do not allow this situation to strip you of your joy. No matter what is happening, however concerned you have been about your brother Epaphroditus, however much you have worried about me, however threatened you feel by my rivals, however much you have suffered at the hands of the enemies of the cross, however debilitating the argument between my two co-workers, I tell you plainly, you can rejoice. In fact, rejoice in every circumstance no matter how painful or difficult. This is not about whether you are happy. God does not guarantee that circumstances will always fall together in such a way that you will be happy. I'm talking about something else, something far more profound. I am talking about a deep-seated, life-pervading joy that comes only in the Lord, no matter what is going on in our world, no matter how difficult things are. So I tell you again, even in the midst of this conflict, rejoice!

Let your gentleness be known to everyone. Treat others with kindness. Don't attack and accuse, even when you are sure you are right, even if what others have done to you is unfair. Put yourself in their world. Listen to them. Respond with gentleness, with soft words and a compassionate heart, even if others shout and accuse. The Lord is near.

Do not worry. Do not allow yourselves to be paralyzed by this situation. Do not allow yourselves to be pulled in two directions. You have resources. You have options. Remember who is in charge. So I urge you to pray. Pray fervently. Don't just list your petitions to God, but also offer your thanksgiving. He has already given you many things, and though you may not recognize it now during this crisis, he is still with you; he still loves you, and he is giving you everything you need. Make sure when you make your requests to him that you include thanksgiving.

When you pray, know who God is and what he will give you. The peace of God that passes all understanding will protect you utterly. God is not offering simply a feeling of wellbeing.

The God of reconciliation has broken in. The peace of God will surround you and shield you. I don't care how damaged the relationship is. God can heal it. God can take you two women with all the difficulties that have surrounded your quarrel, and he can reconcile you in Christ in ways that are beyond your ability to understand.

You may not know how to fix this, but the problem is not beyond God's power. Pray to him. Surrender to him. Take your fractured lives and offer them to him, with thanksgiving. I assure you, the peace of God will safeguard your hearts and your minds in Christ Jesus. It will protect how you think, how you act, and what you say. That, dear Philippians, is good news.

What I will tell you next may be the most difficult thing for you to grasp in this whole situation, but if you will do it, the road to healing will have begun. And what is true for these two women is true for all of you. Euodia, you believe that you are right. You don't think Syntyche understands how much she has hurt you. I know. You may be right. But here is what I want you to do: whenever you look at her, whenever you think about her, whatever in her life is true, whatever is honorable and just—and even you will have to admit that you can name some of these things about her—whatever in her life is pure, if anything about her is pleasing, anything about her that could possibly be commended, anything that is excellent or worthy of praise, I'm going to ask you pointedly, would you focus on those things rather than what she has done to injure you? Would you work out of those interests and concerns?

Syntyche, I will ask the same of you. I am sure Euodia has hurt you. You have blamed her for many things, and you may be right. I know you are carrying a lot of baggage in your relationship and that you feel wounded. But I also believe that when you think about your old friend, you can see good things there, things that are honorable, pure, and pleasing. Would you look at Euodia and see past your pain? If anything about her is commendable, would you consider telling her? If there is anything excellent, anything you can praise, would you concentrate on that so that the gospel can do its work?

Christ is present in both of your lives. If you will stop criticizing and blaming each other long enough to look, you will see him, and you will see the godly qualities he has given each of you. When you think of the other, I am asking you to think about those things. And what is true for these two women is true for the rest of you as well.

Keep doing what is right, the things you were doing when we were all together, the things I taught you, and the life of service I have modeled for you. As you do, accept this promise: the God of peace, the God of reconciliation, the God who heals broken relationships, who desperately seeks his lost children, who calmed the storms and raised his dead son from the grave, this God—no matter how bad you think the situation is, no matter how intractable the conflict, no matter how hurt you feel—this God will be with you.

HEALING AND HOPE

The kingdom of God transcends the small circles of proximity in which we live. Though our own vision may be constricted, God sees beyond our thin experiences and our stunted understanding. He stands above our petty concerns and shortsighted self-interests. He lives and moves in worlds we can hardly imagine. He is invested in the lives of people whose habits and interests we do not care for, whose behaviors we cannot tolerate, and whose attitudes we cannot stomach. He attends to people about whom we cannot marshal even limited concern. Moreover, he sits astride the gulf we have dug between others and ourselves. He refuses to concede that the deep chasm we have cut is permanent or impassable. He has already provided ways to cross over.

God is not the problem, of course. What he wants is clear. We just do not want it as much. We may even find a certain pleasure in the conflict, one we would hate to relinquish. Anger is a pleasing and addictive potion. Feeling victimized provides a certain identity and even power that is hard to give up. Scenes of retribution make stirring dreams in our minds, our tormenters receiving what they deserve, our actions vindicated, our longsuffering rewarded at last. In the long run, of course, anger only wounds us more and makes the healing of our heart as well as the healing of the relationship even more difficult. The question may be, how much do we desire it?

I have always found the healing story at Bethsaida in John 5 disquieting. The man had been ill for thirty-eight years, and Jesus asked him, "Do you want to be healed?" What an odd question to ask a man who had been ill for so long. Surely the answer is obvious. Its presence in the text is disturbing. It is disturbing to me not because I do not understand it, however, rather because I understand it so well. That the man desired to be healed after thirty-eight years is not a given. Being sick was now his identity; it was his entrée into every relationship, the lubricant for every conversation. To be healed was to lose the attention and concern of others. Pain becomes a comfort blanket after a while, and it is hard to give up.

One wonders how much Euodia and Syntyche wanted to be healed. Nursing the wounds caused by the other no doubt provided a certain pleasure. I'm sure they could continue for quite some time wallowing in victimization, enjoying the attention their conflict was causing. But whether or not they sought healing, they needed it. Paul's words to them, to all of them at Philippi, provided the way for them to be healed, and so for us.

Do you want to be healed? Then no matter how intractable the conflict or how painful, whether you have grown weary of it or have found it strangely gratifying, even if the situation has made you sick for thirty-eight years, do not let it rob you of your joy. In the name of Christ, you cannot afford to live in anger, revenge, or self-pity. This is not what the gospel of peace leads to. Because of Christ's suffering work among us, we have received a profound and unfathomable joy. It is not ours to attain, but it is a gift from God. So whatever you do, whatever may happen, however much you may suffer, however unfairly you may be treated, rejoice anyway.

Do you want to be healed? Then be gentle with everyone. It will not seem fair for you to respond with gentleness to someone who treats you with disrespect or rudeness, who baits you or attacks you, or whose tongue is sharp or careless. You will be tempted to lash out, to respond in kind, but doing so will only make you more ill. Stop the escalation. You choose to be gentle no matter what others do. Acting gently is not the same as acting weakly. On the contrary, it places you in the most strategic of positions to do the most good—right next to Christ himself. You may have to act decisively. You may need to remove yourself from a position of vulnerability or abuse. You must not compromise your convictions. But whatever else may happen, make sure that everyone knows your gentleness.

Do you want to be healed? Then don't be paralyzed with anxiety but immerse yourself in prayer. Expend your energy not in fretting over what you cannot control but in opening yourself to the inbreaking of God. Don't be pulled in two directions, but be single-minded in purpose and action. Pray about the conflict. Pray about the other party. Pray for innocent victims. Pray for children and spouses. Pray for the church. Do not simply offer God your petitions, but fill your prayers with thanksgiving. Thank him for what you recognize he has already done and for what he is doing at this very moment that you cannot see. God is at work. His ways may not be visible. His solutions may not be clear. The issues may never be resolved to your satisfaction. Be thankful anyway. Don't be anxious, but devote yourself to prayer.

Do you want to be healed? Then always see the best in everyone. This is not a response of naiveté but of Christian grace. Be wise and discerning, but assume the best in others. Whatever you find that is praiseworthy, praise it. What you see that is excellent, thank God for it. Honor what is honorable. Encourage any evidence of purity. Be careful not to assign motives to the actions of others. Even if your good assumptions prove false and their motives impure, your responses will have flowed from a righteous heart. No matter what, remember that God created the other persons involved; they are precious to him. Whatever reflects his glory in their lives, no matter how small, build on those things.

Finally, recognize that if a way can be created across the chasm between you and others, only God can do it. This is God's work. We are merely his servants, agents for his purpose. How he will accomplish it, we do not know. He may use other people; he may use a variety of circumstances. Through all of these means, he may choose to humble you. Receive his discipline with gratitude. You are not in control, so give it up. He is powerful enough and wise enough to do what is needed. You are not responsible for what others will do, but you can decide how you will act. Your primary task is to surrender to him. As you do, be assured of this great promise: the peace of God will shield your heart and your mind, so be confident. No matter what happens, God himself, the God of peace, will be with you.

Several years ago, a friend told me about a preacher who found himself in the middle of a dispute in his church. I don't know what the issues were. I don't know whether or how much he had contributed to the problem. He had been there for a long time and was approaching retirement age. I suspect some folks were ready for someone else, someone younger, to be their preacher, but I don't know for sure. What I know is that the crisis began to escalate. Phone calls were made, meetings were held, feelings were hurt.

I will never forget what this preacher did. Before things exploded, before sin could wreak havoc on this church, with remarkable gentleness and humility, he stepped down. He refused to blame anyone, he participated in no gossip, and he made no accusations even though several individuals had treated him unfairly. The church had recently lost its custodian and had been looking for another. So he took that job. Other situations would likely have called for different responses. But this man of God preached one week, and the next he was mopping floors and dusting pews. He refused to respond in anger to the mess the church had made. Instead he spent his days on his knees in Sunday School rooms and bathroom floors cleaning other types of messes.

I have a good idea how you want this story to turn out. I assume, like me, you hope that his humility was rewarded and his critics humbled. But this is not a Hollywood movie. Besides, that misses the point. He was not attempting to measure the success of his actions according to prevailing American values. This is not the all-American tale of how the underdog wins in the end. His standards came from a different place. He never preached there again, but he found the resources he needed to love and forgive, to study and pray, to spend time with his family, and to experience great joy in using his broom as he had once used his pulpit: to serve others and bring peace in the name of God.

NOTES

1. Charles Hummel, *The Tyranny of the Urgent* (revised and expanded edition; Downers Grove, IL: InterVarsity, 1999).

2. After writing this section, I discovered a prior use of the phrase "tyranny of the proximate." Journalist Richard O'Mara used it (*The Quill* [June 1985]: 30) to suggest that the increase in foreign news correspondents would not promote greater international awareness but would, rather, accentuate provincialism, a somewhat different argument from what I am making here.

3. All paraphrases throughout the book are mine. In each case I try to summarize the points Paul is making, doing my best to maintain the flow of the argument. I am always aware of the exegetical work that stands behind these paraphrases.

CHAPTER FOUR

CLIMBING THE WALL

Fragmentation in our Churches and in Our Hearts

*Touching the Businesse of the Bounds, which we have now
in agitation; I have thought, that a good fence helpeth to keepe
peace betweene neighbours; but let us take heede that we
make not a high stone wall, to keepe us from meeting.*

—Ezekiel Rogers, in a letter
to John Winthrop (June 20, 1640)

Most children who grow up in suburban America share a common inventory of swimming pool games. Kids everywhere climb on the shoulders of their friends to compete in "Chicken" matches or race along the pool bottom in a game of "Sharks and Minnows" or make the smallest kid cry playing "Keep Away." As long as there are diving boards, poolside parents and sunbathers will have to endure being doused by cannonballs. More than a few high school students in world history are surprised to discover that when the great thirteenth-century European traveler Marco Polo was introduced to the court of the Great Khan, they did not shout "Polo," then run away before he could catch them. Pools large and small, public and private, are mostly the same in regard to their games.

My friends and I, however, played a different game at our local swimming pool growing up. From the time we pulled on our trunks in the dressing room until we jumped into the station wagon for the ride home, we were consumed with one thing. To understand our game, you would have to understand the uniqueness of our swimming pool. I have never heard of another one quite like it. The organizers of the Christian Youth Center, noble in thought and pure in heart, had built a wooden fence down the middle of our pool. Girls swam on one side, boys on the other. Of course, a few lucky pre-school boys got to go with their moms and hang out with the girls, but I suspect they weren't all that excited about it. My pre-adolescent friends and I, however, were completely segregated from all females. Therefore, our primary swimming pool game was "Try to See the Girls."

Both sides of the fence had diving boards, but only ours was used to any great extent. You might be amazed at how high twelve-year-old boys can jump off a diving board when they are highly motivated. We learned to "bounce" each other, two people on the board, the one behind anticipating the jump of the other, providing extra spring therefore extra height. Every now and then one of us actually got a glimpse of a girl on the other side, causing shrieks mostly by the mothers and grandmothers who, for some reason, did not think the game was as fun as did we. Much of my summers were spent in the penalty box after excessive complaints from the other side.

On one occasion, my good friend Danny huddled us together at the deep end of the pool, speaking quietly so the lifeguard could not hear. "There is a hole in the fence," he whispered. We dove down to see. Sure enough, one of the planks of the wooden fence had rotted and broken off. "I'm going through," Danny told us courageously. It never occurred to us that this might actually be dangerous, that Danny, while the skinniest of us all, might get stuck trying to swim through. Nor did we consider the consequences. We were living in the moment. There was a hole at the bottom of the fence.

The rest of us created a diversion by splashing each other near the rope as Danny slid to the bottom of the pool and slithered through the small opening. The rioting started when one of the moms yelled "boy" in much the same way that an ocean swimmer might yell "shark." Little girls and old women began to scream. Teenage girls wrapped themselves in beach towels, pointing and squealing, "There he is!" The fence had been breached. Our serene, all-American summer afternoon had turned into pandemonium, a testament to excessive testosterone and stupidity, a redundancy I am sure.

Nothing about this story should be surprising. Fences separate and people try to break through. It has always been this way. From ancient Sumer to yesterday's repair work at the United States/Mexican border, from Jericho to the Maginot Line, civilizations are marked by fences and walls. Usually, they are designed to keep people out. Beginning in the sixth century b.c.e., ancestors of the modern Chinese began constructing sections of a wall renovated and completed by the Ming Dynasty almost two thousand years later. This Great Wall, the only man-made object visible from the moon, was designed to keep foreigners out. It was mostly successful. The Berlin Wall, on the other hand, was created not to keep people away but to hedge them in. Over its more than twenty-eight years of existence, around five thousand people escaped over or under the wall. One hundred ninety-two people were killed trying to cross. Some walls protect, some walls contain, but all walls divide.

THROUGH HUMAN HEARTS

More permanent and more devastating than walls separating peoples are the walls that wind through human hearts. The works of August Wilson provide a glimpse into a devastating world of walls and fences. Wilson is an American playwright whose works depicting the struggles of African Americans in the twentieth century have won him two Pulitzer prizes. Born Frederick August Kittel in 1945 of a German father and African-American mother, he has traversed a landscape with walls that most white Americans never see.

Largely abandoned by his father, Wilson took his mother's maiden name as a young teenager. When his mother remarried, the family moved to a mostly white neighborhood in Pittsburgh where they encountered severe racial hostility. Bricks were thrown through the window of his home. Racial incidents occurred almost every day. At Gladstone High School, his classmates subjected him to verbal and physical threats. At age fifteen, Wilson completed a term paper on Napoleon. His teacher, not believing a black student could create a well-written paper, accused him of plagiarism. He was suspended. The principal ignored his attempts to come back to school.

Wilson pursued his self-education at the local library where he honed his talent with words. In subsequent years his poetry and plays have provided an articulate voice to the struggles of countless black Americans and have provided a way for whites to see and perhaps understand what it is like to live as the descendents of slaves in this country.

Wilson's first Pulitzer was awarded for his 1983 play *Fences*. The play is set in the 1950s in his native Pittsburgh, between the beginning of the collapse of Jim Crowism and the onset of the Civil Rights Movement. The protagonist, Troy Maxson, and other men of his generation escaped the conditions of sharecropping, living for years in shacks and jail. The character, like many tragic figures in America's past, paves the way for the next generation of blacks, but he never reaps the harvest of his own sacrifice. These are Wilson's words introducing the play:

> Near the turn of the century, the destitute of Europe sprang on the city with tenacious claw and an honest and solid dream. The city devoured them. They swelled its belly until it burst into a thousand furnaces and sewing machines, a thousand butcher shops and bakers' ovens, a thousand churches and hospitals and funeral parlors and moneylenders. The city grew. It nourished itself and offered each man a partnership limited only by his talent, his guild, and his willingness and capacity for hard work. For the immigrants of Europe, a dream dared and won true.
>
> The descendents of African slaves were offered no such welcome or participation. They came from places called the Carolinas and the Virginias, Georgia, Alabama, Mississippi, and Tennessee. They came strong, eager, searching. The city rejected them and they fled and settled along the riverbanks and under bridges in shallow, ramshackle houses made of sticks and tar-paper. They collected rags and wood. They

sold the use of their muscles and their bodies. They cleaned houses and washed clothes, they shined shoes, and in quiet desperation and vengeful pride, they stole, and lived in pursuit of their own dream: That they could breath free, finally, and stand to meet life with the force of dignity and whatever eloquence the heart could call upon.[1]

Fences challenges us to confront the barriers that still exist in the United States, not just in civic life but also in our churches and in our hearts. Our culture is strewn with fences that not everyone can see. And where there are fences, especially invisible fences, there will be some who have power and some who don't.

I have thought a lot over the last several years about how ethnic minorities live in a predominantly white culture. I have read with great interest literature about the Civil Rights period in America, an era I lived through but not with suitable eyes to see. I have experienced nothing in my life like the Montgomery bus boycott. I can only imagine the powerlessness of a teenager being attacked by police dogs in the park or being pushed hard against downtown buildings by the spray of fire hoses. I have no idea what it would feel like to be in a bus during the Freedom Rides as angry people lined the highways shouting obscenities and as men with baseball bats waited at the next bus station, which had been suddenly abandoned by the police. I can hardly grasp what it means to go to a church in which a bomb kills four precious girls as they settle in to their Sunday School room. I do not know this kind of fear. I cannot tell you for sure how I would respond.

I thought a lot about fences several years ago as I sat in the home of an Indian family in Durban, South Africa. Years before, because of the governmental policy of apartheid, everyone of Indian descent had been moved forcibly from their homes. Doctors, lawyers, school teachers had all lost their homes in a virtual pogrom. These families lost almost everything. Their only crime was not being white. I recognize it in my own hometown as I sometimes see Hispanics treated as socially and intellectually inferior, often neglected or ignored. I witnessed it a few weeks ago as I watched an African-American man who was staying in my hotel try to hail a taxi as empty cabs raced by, picking up white folks on the next block. Racial fences are everywhere if a person has eyes to see.

A year ago, I was one of three whites attending a workshop for African-American ministers. Our evening session ended around midnight. Several of us were hungry. We headed out of the hotel toward an all-night eating establishment. Eight of us made the short trek, seven black men and I. Everyone in the group was highly educated, six having doctorates. All were widely respected. Knowing the men as I did, I was oblivious to how they might be seen by strangers. As we approached the front door of the restaurant, one of my friends pulled me back gently and whispered, "Watch this."

We walked through the door and several tables stopped talking, necks craning toward the front door. The hostess took a step back, looking to either side, trying to find her tongue. I was the last one into the lobby. She looked past the others who had walked in first and looked directly at me. "Eight, smoking or non?" she asked me. I was the only one in the group who hadn't known what to expect. For the first time, I felt the emotion in the room. What I couldn't understand was why my friends were not angry. They just shrugged their shoulders. They experience this most days of their lives. I go to restaurants every week. I just don't see the fences.

Walls between people or groups go far beyond ethnic distinctions, of course. We live in a society that is polarized on a variety of levels. As the national temperament has grown hotter and as strongly held opinions about a variety of issues ossify, the walls seem to increase. Establishing walls in this climate is not the province of any particular group or ideology. Apparently in this day, everyone is a builder.

DISCOURSE IN THE PUBLIC SQUARE

Reasoned discourse in the public square seems to be in full-scale retreat. Our nation is polarized not merely into so-called Red States and Blue States but also into Red Truth and Blue Truth. This is more than division reflecting loyalties to Republican and Democratic parties. Deeper undercurrents are at play. The intellectual conflicts in the nation, at their most extreme, pit the instincts of urban centers against rural areas, those of churchgoers against non-churchgoers, marrieds against unmarrieds, the North against the South, the professional classes against the working classes, whites against ethnic minorities, and much more. The tension shows no signs of diminishing.

What is most striking is not the polarization of the citizenry—the country has seen this before—but rather the selectivity of information that limits our ability to process and discern opposing positions. In the day of cable television and the Internet, none of us ever needs to hear the reasoned arguments of those whose opinions differ from ours. We can choose to hear only positions that solidify what we already believe. From Michael Moore to Rush Limbaugh, from MoveOn.org to truthlaidbear.com, between brutish bloggers and pundits with a cause, one-sided arguments and public ridicule have apparently replaced even-handed presentation of issues and genuine respect for opponents.

The airways and ether world are marked by caricature and derision. The audience can spit out the arguments of the other side already pre-chewed and rejected. No one needs to think anymore. No one needs to listen. This is not real public debate but the lampooning of the opposition as public sport. When Jon Stewart of Comedy Central's "The Daily Show," of all people, begs the hosts of CNN's "Crossfire" to have real dialogue about issues rather than the biased but entertaining advocacy of partisan positions, we know the situation is dire.

In such a climate, how people view the truth often determines how they treat those with whom they disagree. In a recent article in *Time*, Nancy Gibbs describes the current American political climate: "The traditional heralds [i.e. mainline journalists] compete with the authors and bloggers and filmmakers and cable barkers and radio rabble-rousers who appeal to those who tailor the news to fit their political niche.... The stakes of the outcome seem to change the rules. If you believe that your children's safety depends on the right guy winning, what tactics can possibly be out of bounds, and what scruples—political or intellectual or legal or journalistic—are more important than ultimate victory?"[2]

For many, this is not just about which position is right but which principles and practices must win. Since the very future of the nation is at stake, many participants in the political process feel justified in employing any means necessary. As a result, the United States has become mired in unparalleled partisanship and intolerance. We live in a nation of walls that are buttressed by our inability, or refusal, to engage in meaningful dialogue with others whose opinions conflict with our own.

BEHIND CHURCH WALLS

Not surprisingly, what is true in American politics is true for many church leaders as well. Rather than engaging in behavior that contrasts with prevailing cultural values, we Christians often use the very tactics employed by secular politicians and journalists. Sometimes our behavior is even worse. Reasoned public discourse in the church about things that matter is rare. People on all sides label and blame. The world is segmented into "us" and "them." We tend to talk only to "our kind of people." We read the books, journals, bulletins, and weblogs of people like us. If we read others, it is often with an eye to beat them or to catch them in a lapse of logic or as an opportunity to discredit them. Since we believe in the inviolability of our own position, we seldom consider the ethics of our behavior. Our eternal ends always seem to justify any means we choose. These sorts of behaviors build higher and stronger fences.

For this and other reasons, the landscape of many cities is littered with churches of every shape and flavor. Especially in the major cities of the Bible Belt, Christians face a veritable smorgasbord of ecclesial practices and beliefs. They seek to attend the kind of church they like, which is to say, a church like them. In such a world, most Christians in the United States never have to be confronted by anyone whose opinions differ substantially from their own. Their church, often chosen because its perspective on virtually every matter concurs with their own, becomes the convenient filter through which they view the neighborhood, the nation, and the world.

In this way, churches reflect the high degree of selectivity typical of our contemporary culture. Out of all the possible churches in our urban and suburban settings, we simply select the one we like in the same way that we might choose *U.S. News and World Report* over *Newsweek,* or Fox News rather than CNN. Or in the same way we might choose ranch dressing over bleu cheese. With so many attractive choices available to us, our task is merely to choose what we are most comfortable with. In this day of hyper-selectivity, genuine discourse is hardly possible because we never have to talk to people whose positions differ substantially from our own. In that environment, changing one's mind because of someone's persuasiveness is unimaginable. If we rarely have relationships with anyone we disagree with, we will be more likely to experience contentment and spiritual equilibrium, an attractive way to live during days of polarization and unrest. Walls are safer and make life in the church more pleasant. Who wouldn't want that?

But as church leaders know, it isn't always this simple. People have minds of their own. Even in those churches where certain positions are enforced, members find ways, however subtle, to express dissent. Good leaders have learned to encourage healthy differences among church members. But sometimes those differences are so profound, the walls so high, that unity within the church is practically impossible. Such is the case for Paul as he addresses a level of polarization between Jews and Gentiles that might even raise our eyebrows.

A WALL OF HOSTILITY

Paul had seen firsthand the hostility between Jews and Gentiles. In an earlier day, as a Jewish leader, he had helped strengthen the wall between them. His very identity had been tied to his Jewishness. Now as a leader within the Christian community, he frequently had to come to grips with the impact of the church's growing diversity. Much of his correspondence addressed the problems that grew out of the multicultural dynamics of the new churches in Asia and Europe. Few issues threatened the future and viability of the church quite as much as this one. As long as the church was a sect of the Jews, a visible manifestation of the true Israel made up primarily of her children, then ethnic conflict would not divide the church. But the moment the door cracked open to allow Gentiles into the assemblies, the trouble would start.

It was not that Paul had a problem with Gentiles as part of the church. On the contrary, he was their defender. He was their apostle. While the Lord had brought Peter unenthusiastically into a broader understanding of a church consisting of all peoples, Paul had been their advocate from the beginning. He and Barnabas defended them at the Jerusalem Council. They argued that Gentiles must not only be accepted into the church, they should be received as equal members, fully brothers and sisters in Christ. But the fact that Paul was their advocate did not mean that he did not grasp the problems that would be created as their proportions in relation to Jewish Christians grew. The wall between Jew and Gentile was high.

We should be careful not to overstate the case here. The Romans were not persecuting Jews. In fact, because so many Jewish soldiers had fought alongside Julius Caesar a century before, their worship was protected by law. Being Jewish was seen by Romans as odd but not illegal. However, Jewish habits, customs, and behaviors were off-putting to many Gentiles. Because of their faith and history, they sometimes came across as overly confident, even arrogant. They often kept to themselves. The most pious of them did not participate in community festivals and ceremonies. While frequently serving in respectable positions in the community, they rarely allowed themselves to be fully absorbed into the culture.

Throughout the empire, their synagogues functioned as Jewish neighborhood centers. These were places of education and community as well as worship. Gentiles generally were excluded from the activities there. Even though Gentile converts were allowed access, they were typically treated as second-class members. Converting to Judaism had advantages, to be sure, but it was not the same as being an ethnic Jew. Besides, there were certain disadvantages to converting, not the least of which was the circumcision required of all male converts. Not surprisingly, many Gentiles, drawn by the Jews' monotheism among other beliefs and practices, nevertheless chose to remain godfearers rather than proselytes. While many Gentiles found Jewish religion attractive, they were often kept at arms' distance by Jewish people.

From the other side, Jews generally saw themselves as superior to Gentiles. They were, after all, descendents of Abraham, the chosen people of God. Their circumcision was a sign of their special relationship with God. They looked down on Gentile morals, the way Gentiles viewed marriage, and the profane way that Gentiles approached family meals. Eating together, for the Jews, was a visible sign of the presence of God, an act of worship and hospitality. Eating together, for Gentiles, was often an opportunity to party, an occasion for drunkenness or worse.

Roman citizens could pride themselves in their laws, their sense of order and efficiency, their armies, and their world domination. Greeks found satisfaction in being the cradle of civilization, the seedbed for science, philosophy, and rhetoric, the intellectual engine for Rome's accomplishments. But the Jews were not intimidated. They knew they were God's very people, children of the promise, close to God's own heart. In cultural and religious pride, they took second place to no one.

In the church, Christian Jews learned to tolerate Gentile converts, but Christianity belonged first of all to the Jews. After all, it was not some new religion that had been established but the culmination of all that God had been doing among the Jews for centuries. The Bible of the church was the Jewish Bible, Scriptures that Jewish Christians already knew well. The stories of God's faithfulness and deliverance had been their stories long before the Gentiles entered the picture. Clearly, the Gentiles had much to learn.

In most churches, the antagonism between the two groups churned just beneath the surface. In some places, the hostility boiled over. A wall ran through their hearts, a wall constructed over centuries. It divided them and isolated them. Its continued presence threatened the very existence of the church.

In Paul's letter to the Ephesians, his declaration concerning the relationship between Jews and Gentiles is striking: "Christ is our peace. In his flesh he has made both groups into one and has broken down the dividing wall that is the hostility between us" (2:14). No matter how strong their differences, no matter how deep the hostility between them, no matter how repulsed they were of each other, how bruised they might have been by things said and done in the church, no matter how unacceptable it might be to the culture around them, Christ has torn down the walls. The walls of animosity, of cultural superiority, and of isolation have been broken. Fences that segregated, that created misunderstandings, that caused each to be afraid, fences between Jewish truth and Gentile truth, between Jewish and Gentile values, have been pulled down. He has made both groups into one.

Paul refuses to accommodate the chasm between them. He does not merely open a gate through the wall so that they might pass through from time to time should they so desire. He does not justify their continued detached existence. He does not advocate some sort of separate but equal relationship because separate is never equal. He will not allow one group superiority over the other. It never occurs to him to let the groups worship according to their own tastes and styles. He does not create an early service for Jews and a late service for Gentiles. Rather, Christ has pulled down the wall between them. They will have to learn to deal with the implications of that. To understand the significance of Paul's rhetoric here, we must place his argument within the context of the whole Ephesian letter. The place that Paul begins is not with walls but with power and powerlessness, though the two issues are inextricably linked.

POWER FOR THE POWERLESS

The letter to the Ephesians is not as personal or intimate as the one to the Philippians. Clearly, Paul did not know these readers. He indicated that he had heard of their faith (1:15), and he assumed they knew some things about his own ministry (3:2, 3) as well as the basic message about Christ (4:21). They were obviously Gentiles (2:11; 3:1), but not ones with whom Paul had a relationship. Perhaps this letter was designed to be circulated among churches in Asia Minor. Perhaps these were Gentiles in Ephesus who were converted after Paul had left the city. Whoever they were, they were trying to live in two worlds, with one foot in the kingdom of God and one foot in the pagan culture.

A prevailing issue in the book is the readers' desire to have sufficient power in order to cope with the powerlessness that was part of the fabric of life in that culture. Like most people in the ancient world, they were concerned about the impact of what they called "the principalities and powers." These were not just governmental powers but the spiritual forces that, they believed, controlled history, the power of the past to affect the future, the might of wealth, the benefits and burdens of law, the place of tradition, the effect of prejudices, and all the conditions that determine whether a person or a household thrived or perished.[3]

From this perspective, humans are at the mercy of spiritual realities living in the heavenly places who have power to make or break us, to give us success or failure, to give us harvest or drought, to cause our children to live or die. How do you placate these spiritual forces or control them so that they will work for you and not destroy you? For many of the Ephesians the answer was, whatever it took. Thus they worshipped the goddess Diana, but they also looked to other resources. Some practiced witchcraft. Others pursued magic.

As many Gentiles in Ephesus became Christians, they did not lose their fear of the powers and principalities. They had confidence in the power of Christ, but they were willing to look for other resources as well. Christ's power might have been greater than all other powers, but that did not mean they couldn't tap into others if the situation warranted it. In this way, they tried to live in two worlds, in the kingdom of God and in Ephesus. They assumed the more power they had, the better they could cope with the spiritual forces of darkness. The Gentiles' unstated question in Ephesians then is this: where will we find the power we need for our threatening circumstances?

Surely at some level we can understand their concern. We may not be tempted to dabble in witchcraft or magic, but any parent of a terminally ill child or any person who was fired from a job unfairly and without recourse understands what it means to feel powerless in the face of an overwhelming situation. All of our instincts are to find some way to fix it, some solution that can make things right.

I know of a boy who was born a number of years ago with cerebral palsy. I can only imagine the sense of helplessness that his parents felt. Even when he was an infant, Robert's parents knew he would never be normal, he would never be able to feed or dress himself or live a regular life. Several of their friends suggested they institutionalize Robert because they would not be able to help him adequately. What person could not understand their desperation, their sense of powerlessness?

When our friend Glyn was diagnosed with ALS, "Lou Gehrig's disease," we were all stunned. She was vibrant, funny, talented. She had a beautiful alto voice and a contagious laugh. We could hardly grasp it. ALS is always terminal. We felt numb and helpless.

All of us can identify, at least a little, with the readers of Ephesians as they tried to cope with their powerlessness in the face of the spiritual forces they believed loomed over them. They felt desperate. They looked for power wherever they could find it. Paul's response would not only shape the church's views toward power, it would serve as the foundation for everything he would say about the wall that existed between Gentiles and Jews.

The language of Paul's opening prayer (Eph. 1:3-14) is rich and complex, and the message is pointed. The subject is "God," the verb is "chose," and the object is "us." Everything else adheres to this basic sentence. God chose us. In his power, in his wisdom and insight, before the foundation of the world, according to his good pleasure, he chose us. The making of the church was not an afterthought; it was not a change of plans after an experiment with Israel had failed. From the very beginning God had the church in his heart, Gentile as well as Jew. But for what did he choose the church? He chose us, Paul says, to be holy and blameless, to live lives distinct from the values of the world. I do not want you living like your pagan neighbors, Paul is implying. God wants you to live differently. How you live matters.

Beginning in 1:15, Paul's language becomes even more pointed. Watch how his argument unfolds, how he addresses the Gentiles' concerns about power and then moves to the larger issue of their place in the kingdom with reference to the Jews.

I have heard about your faith. I am pleased with how you love the saints everywhere. That's why I constantly thank

God for you. But when I pray to him about you, I ask that he would give you discernment and clarity. There are things you still do not understand. I pray that you may grasp the full implications of what you do not yet fully see, that you will understand more fully what your inheritance includes. More specifically, I want you to grasp how powerful Christ is.

You Gentiles are concerned about power, and rightly so. But you have never quite understood the power of Christ. My prayer is that you may know how incredibly great is his power according to the working of his great power.

Surely you can't miss the point I am making. How can I be clearer? All I can do is heap phrase upon phrase so that you will understand: I want you to know the limitless power of his power! Christ's power is enough. No other power can supplement what he alone can give. God put his power to work in Christ when he raised him from the dead, when he seated him at his right hand in the heavenly places.

The power you have at your disposal in Christ is the very power that breathed life in his dead lungs, that rolled the stone away. Moreover, as you feel concern about the powers of the universe who live in the heavenly places, who affect your life and all that happens to you, let me be clear: God has seated the resurrected Christ there in the heavenly places. He is not subject to these powers; he rules them! God has given Christ authority over all the principalities and powers whose control over your life you fear. Christ has power over all the powers in the heavenly places and all the powers on earth, over everyone and everything that would control you.

He has put all things under Christ's authority. He has made Christ the head. But why? For what purpose? He made Christ head over all things for you! You are his body. You are the fullness of Christ. Everything that God has done in Christ he has done for you.

So why would you be afraid of any power? Why would you Gentiles try to live with one foot in an earthly kingdom? Why would you feel a need to look for the same spiritual resources that your pagan friends seek? I'm telling you clearly, Christ's power is enough.

Now, when you lived according to pagan values, when you were dominated by the ruler of the power of the air, you were dead. In your trespasses and sins, you were utterly dead. But God gave you life. More than that, God does not leave us helpless here while Christ reigns from above. He has raised all of us up with Christ and has given us all seats side by side with Christ in the heavenly places.

He has done all this by his grace, in other words as a gift to you, which you received in faith. None of this was your doing. You didn't have the power to accomplish it. Only he does. It should be clear that what he has done for you comes only from him. You have nothing to boast about. You are what he made you to be. You, all of us in Christ, were created for good works. It was his plan from the very beginning that those of us who are in him would be equipped to live rightly, that this would be our way of life.

Many of Paul's readers felt powerless to respond to the spiritual forces of darkness, the principalities and powers. But for Paul, the very powerlessness of the Christian community was an opportunity for the gospel. Because they were not in control of every circumstance, they could utterly rely on Christ. When they were ready to do that, the door would be open for the working of God's power.

Over the years, I have seen the impact of such power in profound ways. For Robert Reid, in spite of his cerebral palsy, in spite of being in a wheelchair every day, of not being able to dress or feed himself, he has lived an extraordinary life: he graduated from college, has a master's degree, is serving as a missionary to Portugal, is a devoted husband and father. He has baptized dozens of people and has planted churches. He has been an inspiration to thousands of people because of his faith and courage. Yet every day he prays a prayer that goes something like this: "Lord, I thank you for this frail body, because in my weakness you work with great strength not for my sake but for your glory." Not just in spite of his weaknesses but because of them, Robert is able to serve the kingdom with power and effectiveness.

Christ's power within us does not mean everything always works out right. Glyn Johnson's disease ultimately took her life, as ALS always does. But Christ was still at work. In my last conversation with her, she told me, "I have prayed constantly for God to heal me. I am convinced he heals in three ways. Sometimes he heals from the outside, through the skills of doctors or the power of medicine. He hasn't healed me in that way. Sometimes God heals from the inside, by miraculously curing a person of their disease. He hasn't chosen to heal me in that way either. But the third way God heals is by taking a person's heart and turning it into the heart of Jesus. He has healed me in that way, and it has made all the difference." The greatest ministry of Glyn's life was in her last months. The impact of her faith has been enormous. Even when she could no longer speak, Christ's power was sufficient for her.

Paul's readers needed healing. Whatever their personal issues, whatever their individual fears in the face of the principalities and powers, the whole church was handicapped. Gentile and Jewish Christians could not seem to work with each other. This was due, at least in part, to the Gentile's attempt to rely on power outside the power of Christ. As long as they were looking for every conceivable resource, they were robbed of the one resource that could actually help them. Christ's power was sufficient for them if they had eyes to see.

Once that dependence on God is established, Paul can attack the wall that divides them. Jew and Gentile are on equal footing. Both are powerless. Both have been chosen by God. Both, in Christ, are seated at God's right hand in the heavenly places. Both have received salvation not according to what they have done but as a gift from God. He addresses his Gentile readers directly, beginning in 2:11:

> Don't forget, you Gentiles, that at one time you were without Christ. Remember you were not a part of God's special relationship with his children, Israel. You were not recipients of the covenant; you were outsiders; you had no hope; you were

without God in the world. The wall between you was real.
You were not a part of God's family.

But now those of you who were far off have been
brought near by the blood of Christ. What Christ did in his
death, he did not do only for the Jews. He also did it for you.
Christ is our peace. In his flesh he has made the two groups,
Jew and Gentile, into one. He has broken down the dividing
wall between us. He has destroyed the hostility that separated
us. He made one new humanity in place of the two, thereby
making peace.

So for you Gentiles who have been far off, he proclaims
peace. For us Jews who have been close to him all along, he
proclaims peace. Both of us have equal access to the Father
through Christ. Therefore, no matter what your customs and
history, no matter how you dress or what you eat, no matter
how odd your accent or how strange your native language, no
matter how far away you were—how disobedient, how sinful,
how powerless, how hopeless—you are no longer outsiders.
You are citizens of God's house. Christ Jesus himself is the
cornerstone. Because of him, the whole house is joined together,
Jew and Gentile. He is making of us a holy temple. He is
building us together into a dwelling place for God.

So here is my prayer for you. If Christ is the head over all
things, if he is seated in authority in the heavenly places and if
you have been seated with him there, if the wall between you
and the Jews has been torn down so that all of you have access
to the power of Christ, then I pray that you may receive all the
power you need from the inside out, that you may be given
strength through God's Spirit, and that Christ may live in your
hearts as you receive him through faith. I pray that you will
have the power to comprehend and to experience fully the love
of Christ and that you will be filled with all the fullness of God.

Both Jew and Gentile had reason to be confronted by what
Christ had done to their ethnic and cultural identities. Christ's
power was sufficient to tear down the dividing wall between them.

As God's wisdom was revealed in rich variety, so his household reflects that variety. In Christ, Jews are not superior to Gentiles, nor are Gentiles superior to Jews. All are fellow heirs. Now that this foundation has been laid, Paul calls them to live like it.

ONE BODY, ONE BAPTISM

The opening verses of Ephesians 4, where Paul describes the sevenfold oneness of Christ, are familiar to most Christians. There is one body, one spirit, one hope, one Lord, one faith, one baptism, and one God. I have heard this passage most of my life but rarely in context. Mostly I heard two of the seven. There is one body, which is to say one church. There are not many churches—Baptist, Presbyterian, Methodist, Catholic, and Church of Christ—only one church, our church. Since we are the only ones with the right name, the right organization, the right plan of salvation, and the right acts of worship, we are the one church of Ephesians 4. And there is one baptism, not believers baptism and infant baptism, only one. There is one baptism, not immersion and sprinkling, just immersion. The one baptism of Ephesians 4 is the one we practice.

Baptism of believers by immersion can be defended for many reasons and out of numerous passages. And I can affirm Churches of Christ in countless ways. But it is not fair to try to make this text say what it could not possibly have meant. Paul was not addressing a local Church of Christ that was being beleaguered by competing congregations of Presbyterians and Baptists. He was not attempting to take sides in denominational claims and issues that would not appear for hundreds of years. Nor was that church threatened by an incursion of infant baptizers. We should apply this text in ways that reflect what it meant to its original readers. Hear how Paul argues, beginning in the opening verses of Ephesians 4, within the context of the ethnic divide that serves as a backdrop to the entire letter:

> I urge you, I beg you to lead lives worthy of the calling to which you have been called. Life in the church is difficult. I understand that Jews and Gentiles have great differences. But no matter what, treat other people with humility and gentleness.

Be patient. Bear with everyone in love. Use all the energy you have to maintain the unity of the Spirit. The bond you will receive will be peace itself.

There are not two bodies, a Jewish body and a Gentile body. There is one body, one family of believers, one community of faith, one church. It is the same church for both Jews and Gentiles. You are not indwelled by different spirits, one Jewish and one Gentile. There is one Spirit. You do not have separate hopes based on your cultural preferences and expectations. You share the same hope. There is one Lord, not two. You do not exhibit a Jewish faith and a Gentile faith. There is one faith. You weren't baptized with separate baptisms, one Jewish, one Gentile. You were washed clean by the same baptism. You don't proclaim separate Gods in your worship, but there is one God of all, one God above all of you, through all of you, and in all of you. That's where your unity comes from.

You have been given different gifts, but they were all given for the work of ministry. They were given so that the whole body would be built up, not just people you know or people you agree with, and they were given until you come to full unity of the faith, until you truly know the Son of God, until you grow up to the full stature of Christ. Christ is the head of the body, but the body is interconnected, even Jews and Gentiles. You are joined together by every ligament so that every part works right, so that the body will grow, so that the body might be built up by love.

Here then is the basis for unity. Here is the essential message of Ephesians. We don't have to go looking for some other power to get things fixed and get our lives together. Christ is enough. Through Christ God saved us as a free gift. Through his spirit we have been healed so that our hearts are transformed into the heart of Jesus. God has taken our weak bodies, our frail churches, and is using them for his glory. For that reason, we should stop living like pagans. God has given us the power to live as his children. But we can't do it if we are at odds with each other. Being separated from people for whom

Christ died is not living a life worthy of what Christ has done. Whatever separates us Christ has torn down. The dividing wall has been razed. Hostilities have ceased. We are part of the same body, share the same baptism, have the same hope, and worship the same God. Therefore, we should work together, encourage one another, and build one another up so that the work of the church gets done.

Everything else that Paul says in this letter grows out of this foundation. The last half of chapter 4 and first part of chapter 5 describes the pagan behavior they should avoid and the Christian behavior they should employ. As with several other epistles in the New Testament and as is common in ancient letters, Paul includes a household code, a list of instructions for husbands and wives, parents and children, masters and slaves. But he frames them all by saying "be subject to one another out of reverence for Christ" (5:21). All in the church, in other words, should look for ways to serve and honor the others rather than seeking honor for themselves. Husbands are to love their wives, giving up their lives for them as Christ did for all of us. Wives, similarly, are to submit to their husbands as to the Lord. This is the way the whole church should act towards one another. Children should obey parents. Fathers should not provoke their children. Slaves and masters should serve and not threaten; they should treat one another honorably. This is what Christians do, they serve rather than seeking to be served. They look out for each other's interests.

We are not fighting against flesh and blood, Paul says (6:12). At least we shouldn't be. We are not each other's enemies. Attacking each other when the powers of the universe are massing against us is not good strategy, much less good faith. Paul urges us to be equipped for the battle, protected with truth, righteousness, the gospel of peace, faith, salvation, and the Spirit (6:13-17), proper armor for battle but only if Christ fights with us, and only when the enemies are Christ's, not our own.

BROKEN WALLS, BROKEN CHRISTIANS

I know of few differences among modern Christians as profound as the differences between ancient Jews and Gentiles. Yet Paul expected them to work side by side with each other, to submit to one another, to serve and honor and encourage each other because of what they shared in Christ. Early Christians had many ways to witness to the power of Christ within their pagan context, but few could compare to the witness of Jews and Gentiles working together arm in arm for the sake of the kingdom. This is Paul's breathtaking vision in his letter to the Ephesians. It is God's vision for us as well. From this letter many lessons could be applied to contemporary churches, but two are especially needed.

First, in a day when public rhetoric is narrow and partisan and constructive discourse has largely been abandoned, the church must look elsewhere for its models of effective and appropriate communication. A half century ago, even though opinions about national issues were as sharply drawn as they are today, public discourse among statesmen and lawmakers was possible, if not common. Today constructive public discourse is painfully rare.

Rather than serving as a contrast to the prevailing culture, however, contemporary Christian rhetoric often reflects the public marketplace. Not only are we speaking more sharply to one another, we are listening less. When we have to communicate at all, we believe we can afford to close our ears to those with whom we disagree because all that matters ultimately is whether we have the support of our niche group. Moreover, our sources of information and influence are growing increasingly narrow. We hardly read any of the same things, hardly go to the same lectureships or talk in the same circles. We experience little cross-fertilization of ideas. Meaningful dialogue among people of integrity is rare among Christians who share significant disagreements.

Paul has a different view of things. For him church is not a self-selecting gathering of people whose opinions about important issues mostly agree, a place of refuge from uncomfortable conversations. Rather, church is a God-selected gathering of people whose opinions about important issues are diverse, a place of keen dialogue and significant discourse. The purpose of our coming together is to build one another up, to equip one another. It is to make connections and to help each other grow up. It is about Jews sitting down and listening to

Gentiles and caring what they think and who they are. It is about Gentiles speaking with gentleness and humility to Jews because they share the same hope and the same future. It is about powerless people finding power at the most unexpected place, at the place that symbolizes utter powerlessness to both Jews and Gentiles: a cross. There, in an act of seeming powerlessness, God was most vitally at work. While Jesus' hands were nailed to a tree, they were most able to touch and help. At the place of his death, he was most able to mediate life.

Paul called his readers to the cross not only to discuss their salvation, how they had been dead in their trespasses but now were made alive together in Christ, but also to tell them how they should treat one another. Christ gave his life for you, he tells them; therefore submit to one another out of reverence for him. Because of the cross, communication in the church is not about winning but about serving. It is marked by grace. It is driven by humility. It is carried with gentleness. It is bathed in patience. Its purpose is to encourage. Its means is love. Its goal is the maturity of the whole church. Therefore, godly people communicate with each other in healthy ways so that the church is made whole and God's purposes are not hindered.

Second, more than just encouraging healthy communication, Paul is urging his readers to bridge the dividing walls, to be a people who aggressively promote peace. We live in a time in which differences can mostly be avoided. In a culture dominated by choice, we are free to be only with people like ourselves. If we don't like things in our group, we can easily find another that is more to our suiting. And, of course, we can criticize the ones we don't like. Paul might say to churches like ours, maybe it's time to grow up, to become mature to the measure of the full stature of Christ.

We gather with our own people each Sunday, meeting in mostly segregated churches, and we witness to the world that Christians from different races can't find a way to be in godly relationship. We can go to school together and work at the same office, we can play games together, eat at the same restaurants and attend the same events—our national values have pushed us this far—but we can't worship together or share the meal of the Lord. I watch white and black Christians pass each other on the same sidewalk with no nod of recognition. I know many white families who have never had a Hispanic or African-American friend in their home. I know many Christians who live their entire lives without any real relationships with people outside their own race. In a country that prides itself in being a melting pot but which more closely resembles a tossed salad, the church has an opportunity to serve as a witness—people of every race and culture working together for the sake of the kingdom. But each week we continue our separate lives and our separate worship. We have lost sight of our common faith, our common hope, our common baptism, and our common Lord.

Beyond ethnic differences, people of different opinions concerning disputable matters can learn to be together. We can learn to serve one another and work side by side. We can listen and even disagree in a spirit of love and humility. We can worship together, sitting on the same pew, singing the same songs, offering an amen to the same prayers, and eating around the same table. We may have substantial differences, but Christ is powerful enough to make us his people anyway.

Our task is not to choose our brothers and sisters; our task is to love them. Christ's power is enough to traverse the differences. The power that called the universe into being with a single word, that parted the waters of the sea, that caused the Son of God to be born of a Jewish virgin, that defeated the powers of sin and death on a Roman cross, that rolled the stone away from a tomb now empty, that power is enough to take people who disagree or who don't even like each other and make them into the very people of God.

No wall is so high that Christ cannot level it. No gulf is so vast that Christ cannot bridge it. No wound is so deep that Christ cannot heal it. No sin is so great that Christ cannot forgive it. He transcends our barriers of race and culture. He animates our instincts for compassion and care. He crushes our rationalizations and excuses. He brings our hostilities to an end. Christ has empowered us to live no longer as strangers but as citizens of the same kingdom, members of the same family. We may not be able to envision how our enemies could become our friends, how we could ever love people who appear so foolish or whose behavior is so distasteful. We may not be able to picture a church full of people who don't look like us or think like us. We may not be able to imagine a church with Jews and Gentiles, Blacks and Whites, wealthy and poor, masters and slaves, Democrats and Republicans, Hispanics and Anglos, traditionalists and progressives working side by side and worshipping voice by voice. But God does. That is precisely what he sees. That is what he has made. And just over the wall is such a church.

Frank O'Connor, the Irish writer, tells a story about how as a boy he and his friends would make their way across the countryside. When they came to an orchard wall that seemed too high to climb, when they were too doubtful to try so that their journey seemed to be at an end, they would take off their caps and toss them over the wall. Then the boys had no choice but to follow them.

We have come to a wall that seems too high to climb. We cannot figure our way over. We cannot seem to find a foothold. Perhaps today is the day that we come to the wall with our caps in our hands.

Notes

1. August Wilson, *Fences* (New York: New American Library, 1986).

2. Nancy Gibbs, "Blue Truth, Red Truth," *Time*, September 27, 2004.

3. For a fuller discussion, see Markus Barth, *Ephesians: Introduction, Translation, and Commentary on Chapters 1-3*. The Anchor Bible Commentaries (Garden City, New York: Doubleday, 1974), 174.

CHAPTER FIVE

SANCTUARIES OF WELCOME

Where Baptism Leads to Holiness

Let us, before all words, astound them by our way of life.

—John Chrysostom

Alienation and death are the end if we persist in doggedly hanging on to the old ways. Life is the end if we are willing to turn around and let go—to risk being the empty tombs we become in baptism.

—Caroline Westerhoff

I sat Scott down on the front pew as the small crowd began to gather. It was a cool spring Saturday night. We were expecting perhaps twenty people from the singles ministry to arrive for the baptism. I had baptized many people over the years, but this was Scott's first. I was the one, however, who was nervous.

I had talked to Scott by phone the night before. He lived several hours away. His older sister Elaine had called to tell him the good news that she was going to be baptized and asked if he would baptize her. He would, of course, but he wanted to know more about the situation. He was a new Christian himself. He didn't want his sister joining some cult group, so he interrogated me over the phone about my beliefs, about what Elaine understood, what she had been taught. Satisfied, he made his arrangements and met us at the building the next evening.

Scott's concerns were about why Elaine was being baptized. I, already confident of Elaine's understanding, was more concerned about immediate issues, like whether this young man had a clue what to do when he and his sister got in the water. Like a good minister I wanted everything done right, done appropriately.

"How many baptisms have you performed?" I asked him.

"None." This was the answer I was expecting.

"How many have you seen?"

"One. Just my own." Chills went down my back.

"Okay," I said, "let me tell you a few things you should know." I tried to tell him how to stand in relation to his sister, what to say, how to hold her wrists, how to help her hold her nose when she went under, practical things, important things. He wasn't interested. He waved me off.

"I know how to do it," he said, and that was that. My anxiety increased.

We gathered everyone on the stage next to the baptistry. I watched from the wings as Scott met Elaine in the water. They hugged. They stood together facing her Christian friends who watched expectantly from a few feet away. He wasn't positioned next to her correctly, I observed astutely, and he wasn't holding her wrists. My anxiety was off the charts.

"So, Elaine, why are you doing this?" Scott asked her. I groaned audibly. This wasn't it. He hadn't asked the right question. I should have coached him more. I should have insisted he listen to me.

Elaine began to speak. For several minutes she told her story. She confessed her sins with almost shocking frankness. She spoke of when and why she had walked away from God, of her spiritual awakening, of her faith, of her need to have her sins washed away, of her expectation of receiving the Holy Spirit as a companion and help, and of her desire truly to be God's daughter. No one dared to breathe. When she was finished, Scott just said, "I'm gonna baptize you now," and he gently pushed her under. She erupted from the water with a cry of joy.

As I watched the hugs and tears over the next several minutes, I couldn't help but thinking that Scott had gotten it right. He had understood. He had seen more than I. I was concerned about the externals, about things going smoothly, about doing things appropriately. That evening I had been more interested in baptismal manners than in baptismal theology. I had so focused on the how that I had forgotten the why.

An Unholy People Made Holy

I am not the only one who has fallen into this trap, of course. In the history of the church, there have always been those who focused more on the externals of baptism than its meaning. In the fourth century, for example, the Donatists refused to acknowledge the legitimacy of baptisms performed by church leaders who had forsaken the faith during the persecution of the emperor Diocletian a few years earlier. In this case they believed that the past apostasy of the baptizers cancelled out the faith and obedience of the ones being baptized. Or in another example, Charlemagne subdued the Saxons in 772 by, among other means, forcibly baptizing perhaps 100,000 people under penalty of death. He assumed that as long as the right people performed the baptisms in the right way, then God took care of the rest.

In substantially smaller ways, I have experienced this misdirected emphasis on externals. I know of one preacher who baptized a teenager three times because during the first two times a body part had inadvertently come out of the water, a knee or a finger, so that the body wasn't all immersed simultaneously. A member at one of the churches where I used to preach expressed concern about the salvation of people I had baptized because I did not wear a coat and tie in the water and mostly because I didn't raise my right hand during the baptisms as all the previous preachers there had done. These are extreme views, to be sure, but they are different not in kind but in degree from how baptism is sometimes viewed.

This focus on the external characteristics of baptism, the how and when, comes naturally to those of us who are part of churches in the Stone-Campbell Restoration Movement. This emphasis in many ways differentiated us from other groups. Our identity emerged on the frontier of nineteenth-century America at least partially in response to the baptismal beliefs and practices of two traditions.

First, restoration churches distinguished their theology of baptism from that of the Protestant churches of Europe that played a key role in America's early development. Since the time of Constantine, European nations grew to connect baptism with civil life in such a way that baptismal records functioned almost analogously to modern birth certificates. To argue against baptizing babies, as the Anabaptists had done in the sixteenth century, was for many European church and government officials more than just a threatening doctrine. It was tantamount to promoting civic chaos. Infant baptism was the norm for all the state churches. On American soil, restoration churches rejected this practice, not because it was unnecessary for civic life in a country not bound by state religion, but because it did not reflect the teaching of Scripture or the practice of early Christians. They insisted on baptizing only believers.

Second, restoration churches contrasted themselves with churches late in the nineteenth century that disconnected baptism from salvation altogether. If God did the saving, some argued, then no human work could inaugurate that redemptive activity, including baptism. Salvation then came at the confession of faith; baptism was merely a visual sign of what God had already done. Eventually some churches in America ceased practicing baptism altogether or relegated it to a secondary role; the moment of salvation was one's public expression of faith such as reciting the "sinner's prayer." In contrast, restoration churches continued to connect salvation and baptism, as the great tradition of Christianity had done through the centuries. They taught, and still teach, that baptism is decisive in the faith response of believers, connecting believers to the blood of Jesus and allowing them to experience God's saving work.

All restoration churches share this commitment to baptism. If many restoration churches have a problem, however, it is not that we teach too much about being baptized but that we teach too little about living as baptized people. This disconnection between baptism and holiness is evident in a variety of ways. I have seen it in churches that are baptizing children at younger and younger ages so that baptism is not viewed against the background of the insidious power of sin but as a public affirmation of the sweet behavior of children who have barely left infancy. I have seen it in churches that have grown too sophisticated to talk much about baptism or who deemphasize it because they don't want to isolate themselves from other religious groups or appear judgmental. I have seen it in churches that send campaigners to other countries, baptizing people after little instruction, then returning home with an impressive headcount while the people represented by those statistics return quickly to their old beliefs and practices. I have seen it among those who talk about baptism as if it were little more than a legal transaction in heaven, God transferring the names of the immersed from the debit side of the divine ledger to the credit side. From this perspective, baptism is a human work, a culminating step among several steps by which those who were lost become saved.

The disconnection between the event of baptism and the practice of holy living is evident in the behavior of some church leaders who preach that baptism is crucial for salvation but apparently not crucial to empower Christians to act kindly and peaceably towards others. It is revealed in the cynicism of those whose education and theology have pushed them away from legalism and sectarianism but not away from unholy talk, relentless criticism, and smug superiority. It shows itself in the congregational life of churches that insist on baptism but who disregard Christians of different races, who tolerate racist comments among members, and who could never imagine showing hospitality to people of other ethnic groups or to those of radically different social classes. More broadly it is evident in the careless talk, gossip, and divisive behavior that is too common in the very churches that insist on baptism's importance. The irony is conspicuous. To borrow a metaphor, some have been so preoccupied with the wedding, making sure it was done right and the wedding certificate signed and filed at the courthouse, that they have overlooked the marriage itself. Those who have should not be surprised at how poorly things turn out.

My concerns here are not that we emphasize baptism less but rather that we emphasize it more. I believe that had we done so all along, had we understood what kind of people God made us in our baptism, our churches wouldn't be so fragmented. How could baptized people engage in destructive behavior? How could we disparage or ignore people for whom Christ died? How could those of us who are washed by the blood of Jesus sully his name by our words and actions?

If we were more alert to the sanctifying work of the resurrected Christ whom we put on in baptism, we would treat one another differently. We would be more patient and kind. We would be godlier. That is to say, we would be changed. What we experience in Christ is not merely some accounting entry in the heavenly realms but a blood-drenched transformation of the human condition here and now. Christ changes how we think, how we act, what we say, and how we treat others. He gives us new eyes and a new heart. We are by God's power unholy people made holy.

Being right about baptism is not merely about getting the chronology of the salvation event right. It is knowing what baptism means and what is accomplished in it. Even then, our understanding of baptism's purpose and outcome is not what makes it effective. God is the one who works in baptism, not we, and his work within us changes everything. During days of conflict, our common baptism should be our best resource. It should bring us together rather than tear us apart. Baptism, rightly seen, is God's great uniter. All of us meet him there in our sins. All of us are made clean in its waters. It is the place of our surrender. It is the wellspring of our hope. How could we divide what Christ gave his life for?

A GIFT FOR THE COLLECTION

The connection between baptism and holiness is a common theme in the New Testament. The various writers, in the context of troubled or divided churches, do not argue about whether baptism is necessary. Such a question about baptism would not emerge until more modern times. First-century believers, if asked "Does a person have to be baptized to be saved?" would be baffled. They would hardly be able to understand what was behind such a question. All believers were baptized. Why would anyone not be? The New

Testament discusses baptism not primarily in order to demonstrate its role in the process of salvation but as an appeal to Christians to live by its power and promise.

Such is the case in Romans 6, one of the most substantial discussions about baptism in the New Testament. This chapter contains some of the most familiar words about baptism in the entire Bible. But anyone who has read it carefully understands that Paul is not so much arguing for baptism as he is arguing from it. Baptism here is not a conclusion but a premise. It is assumed. They were all baptized, but what does their baptism mean? How does it inform their understanding of sin and grace? What are its consequences? How does it call them to live?

To begin to answer these questions, we must understand the larger purpose of the letter and how this material fits into Paul's overall argument. Romans 6 is not a reflective essay on the theme of baptism. Moreover, the epistle itself is not a general theological exposition or, in the words of Martin Luther's associate Philipp Melanchton, "a compendium of the Christian religion." It is not an essay concerning justification by faith detached from specific historical circumstances however extensively this important doctrine is discussed in the letter. Rather, Romans is an immensely practical letter to a specific church threatened by fragmentation due to ethnic, cultural, and theological differences. For this reason, Paul's message is especially relevant to contemporary churches that are experiencing suspicion, gossip, unhealthy talk, polarization, and division.

The fundamental issue in Romans, as it was in Ephesians, is a clash between Jewish and Gentile Christians that threatens to undermine the mission of the church. Paul's concerns in this regard dominate his arguments throughout the four major sections of the letter. In chapters 1-4 it drives the discussion of how the righteousness of God affects both Jews and Gentiles, all of whom are sinners. In chapters 9-11 it dominates the complex arguments about Gentiles being grafted on to the Jewish vine and whether Israel will be saved. It stands behind the practical exhortations in chapters 12-16, implicitly in the detailed instructions of 12-14 concerning the strong and the weak, and explicitly in chapter 15 as Paul makes clear his purpose for writing. The differences between Jews and Gentiles serve as an important grid in understanding the extensive list of personal greetings in chapter 16. Though the divisions between Jewish and Gentile Christians is not overt in the breathtaking language of chapters 5-8, Paul's arguments in these chapters provide the crucial theological lens through which his ultimate point must be understood.

The immediate context of the letter, at least in part, grew out of the great changes that had occurred among the house churches scattered throughout the city just a few years before the letter was written. More than likely the church had been established in Rome primarily by Jewish Christians who had immigrated there from across the empire. No apostle had established the church in Rome. Not surprisingly, as these Christian communities largely revolved around synagogues, Jewish Christians dominated the leadership. But things changed significantly in the year 49. The Roman historian Suetonius describes some sort of disturbance among Jews in the city caused by a certain "Chrestus," more than likely a reference to the proclamation of Jesus by some of the Jewish Christians. Whatever the specific cause, an edict by Emperor Claudius caused the expulsion of many Jewish Christians, including Aquila and Priscilla (Acts 18:2). By the time the Jews were able to return upon Claudius' death in 54, life in the church had changed irrevocably. Now Gentiles, not Jews, dominated the Roman church. Their centers of influence were house churches scattered throughout the city, not synagogues. These house churches would have functioned quite differently from what the Jewish Christians would have known. Among other things, they would not have been restricted by Jewish dietary laws or the keeping of certain Jewish holy days. By itself this shift would have brought a measure of tension. Into this context Paul wrote his letter to the Christians in Rome.

Paul's long salutation in Romans 16 provides some hints about the makeup of the Christian community when Paul writes. Some of the names are Jewish; most are Greek. At least three and as many as eight house churches can be discerned.[1] These churches more than likely grouped themselves around ethnic and cultural identities. While sharing the same overall purpose and mission, they would likely have met separately, aggravating the suspicions and amplifying the differences.

The divisions evident among the Jewish and Gentile Christians in Rome are a microcosm of what was taking place throughout the empire. Whether Jewish Christians were the dominant group among churches, as was the case of the readers of Paul's letter to the Galatians, or whether Gentiles were predominant as in Rome, suspicion and distrust were abundant. Paul's mission, of course, was primarily to Gentiles. From the very beginning when he and Barnabas argued on behalf of Gentile converts at the Jerusalem Conference in Acts 15, Paul had staked everything on the inclusion of Gentiles in the community of believers. As he wrote Romans, he did not know whether his ministry had been in vain.

Paul indicates one of the primary purposes of his letter in 15:15, 16. I have written this letter boldly to you, he says, "because of the grace given me by God to be a minister of Christ to the Gentiles in the priestly service of the gospel of God, so that the offering of the Gentiles may be acceptable, sanctified by the Holy Spirit." He had hoped to come to Rome but had been delayed collecting money to help take care of the poor among the saints in Jerusalem (15:22-26). This is not the only place we read that Paul gathered an offering for Christians in Jerusalem. He spent several years gathering a collection for Jewish Christians, mostly from Gentile churches.[2]

This is no incidental collection. It is not merely that Jerusalem Christians were in need and Gentile churches had an opportunity to give. The significance of the collection is far greater than that. Paul is concerned that the collection itself would create a deep fissure within the church. Would Jewish Christians receive this offering? The answer to this question is not as obvious as modern readers might think, and as Paul writes Romans, he doesn't know how it will turn out. If the Jerusalem Christians accept the gift, they would by so doing accept Gentiles openly as brothers and sisters, fellow heirs to all of God's promises. A rejection of the gift would mean a rejection of the Gentiles and the Gentile mission, a development with serious consequences for the future of the church.

Paul's entire ministry is on the line. God had called him to engage in priestly service to the Gentiles, serving as a sort of midwife for them into the kingdom of God. Paul tells the Romans, I am very anxious to come to Rome, but I won't do so until I complete this ministry. I beg you to pray about all this so that I will be rescued from the unbelievers in Judea and that my service to Jerusalem may be acceptable to the Christians there (15:30, 31).

The church in Rome would be crucial to his efforts. Paul needed their prayers and support for the collection. More than that, he needed their assistance and encouragement for his planned mission to Spain (15:22-24). A divided church in Rome would undermine the work of God throughout the empire.

Many modern scholars agree that a significant local problem had erupted in the Roman church, the specifics of which are found in 14:1-15:13. Others suggest that this is a general argument reflecting problems in churches throughout the empire rather than being an acute issue in Rome. I am inclined toward the former. Paul's teaching is clear either way. The particular concerns are about the keeping of dietary laws and observing certain holy days. Some, presumably Jews, wouldn't eat certain meats or drink wine, and they kept a Jewish calendar in observing certain special days. Others, more than likely the Gentiles who had become predominant in the church over the past few years, had no problem with eating and drinking and were not inclined to keep the Jewish holy days. This extensive discussion reveals an issue of great volatility and one that is symptomatic of the larger rift between Jewish and Gentile Christians everywhere.

Everything Paul says early in the epistle serves as a foundation for his exhortations about Christian unity at the end. The book is not an abstract essay about faith and works but an apostolic intervention in a local church that has profound implications for all churches everywhere. The overriding question in Romans is, can Jewish and Gentile Christians with their significant differences be part of the same church?

This is a question of profound importance for churches in the twenty-first century. Can Christians who disagree with one another worship together? Can they work side by side in a common cause? Are the only two options either to agree or leave? In one congregation I know, a group of people who are unhappy with the direction of the church gather each week in their own Sunday School class. Most weeks the discussion is oriented around the complaints of one or more of the members. One of the elders quietly refers to the group as the "Dissenters Class." I wonder if disagreement could be handled more constructively. What choices are available to the elders other than "let them complain" or "shut them down"? The question Paul faced regarding the Christians at Rome reflects well our own tensions: can Christians who disagree profoundly with one another be part of the same church?

SIN AND THE RIGHTEOUSNESS OF GOD

To understand how Paul argues for the specifics of Christian unity in the last part of the letter, we need to see the basis for unity as he unfolds it in the rich and powerful language of the early chapters. The theme of Romans 1-4, though complex in language and implication, might be summed up simply. The righteousness of God has been revealed to everyone, both Jews and Gentiles. Since all are separated from God by their sins, neither Jews nor Gentiles can boast. Salvation has been accomplished entirely by the power of God.

He states this theme in 1:16, 17. The gospel is God's power for salvation to everyone who has faith. That is, God's power has not been given only to one group but to all, Jews as well as Greeks. He makes clear to his Gentile readers, who now dominate the Roman church, that they have much indebtedness to the Jews. God's righteousness, his covenant faithfulness, has been offered to both peoples. He loves all of them.

He restates this theme in 3:21, 22: "the righteousness of God has been disclosed...the righteousness of God through faith in Jesus Christ for all who believe." God was faithful in making and keeping his covenant for the sake of everyone, not just for Jews but also for Gentiles. Between these framing statements in chapters 1 and 3, Paul describes how both groups have sinned, the Gentiles apart from the law (1:18-32) but also the Jews for whom God's will was made clear

(2:1-3:20). We Jews are not better off than you Gentiles, he says, because both groups are under the power of sin (3:9).

In other words, neither group can claim superiority. Both Jews and Gentiles stand before God as sinners. None of them are justified by what they have done but by trusting what Christ Jesus has done (3:24-27). So how could any of them brag about what they brought to the table, about their place or position?

Further, Paul says that the righteousness of God has been at work among both Gentiles and Jews. Abraham was viewed by God as righteous not because he was circumcised but because of his faith. This happened before he became a Jew, so to speak, before he was circumcised. His faith was counted as righteousness not because of his ethnic group or because of his circumcision but because of his faith, and the same is true for all his spiritual descendants, both Jew and Gentile (4:9-12, 22-24). Neither group is in a position to judge the other.

Here is the beginning of Christian unity. It does not begin with human planning, intellect, or will but with God himself. The gospel creates unity. We are sinners all—Jew and Gentile, strong and weak. None of us deserves to be in relationship with God. But the righteousness of God has broken in; therefore, we have peace in him. On the basis of this argument, Paul will ultimately be able to say: if our righteousness comes from God, if he has established our peace, what right do we have to fight or condemn each other? In this the groundwork for unity is laid.

In chapters 5-8 Paul largely restates the ideas of 1-4 but approaches them with a different thrust. He introduces the major ideas of this section in chapter 5 and restates and expands them in chapter 8. In the first four chapters, human sin and God's righteousness are the themes of a somewhat formal argument in which the readers' identity as Jews and Gentiles is the primary focus. Here their identity as Jews and Gentiles is beside the point. They are all participating in nothing less than a cosmic shift from the old order to the new, from the reign of death begun in Adam to the reign of life ushered in by Christ (5:12-21). They are living in the labor pains of a new age, from one dominated by sin and death to one set free by the death of God's son, lived in the Spirit (8:1-30). From this standpoint their disputes about dietary practices and holy days should shrink into insignificance. They are participating in a change of cosmic order, of the battle between flesh and Spirit.

In such a world, at least two things are clear. First, they should expect to suffer (5:3, 8:18). Even in their suffering, however, the Holy Spirit is present in their groanings and pleads for them with God, who graciously intercedes on their behalf (5:5; 8:26, 27). Second, if they are to boast about anything, it is not in themselves but in their hope (5:2-5; 8:18-25). While they may be caught in this cosmic battle between death and life, God is nevertheless at work. They can have confidence in him and not shrink back in fear. As God's children they can approach him as "abba," fellow heirs with Christ (8:14-17). Moreover, however much they may suffer, God is causing everything to culminate for the ultimate good of everyone who loves him (8:28). No matter what happens to them, they will never be separated from Christ's love (8:31-39). Therefore they hope.

These themes of suffering and hope, of death and life, of the old order and the new, dominate the bookend arguments of this section, chapters 5 and 8. In the middle lie two chapters in which Paul vividly portrays life between the ages. In chapter 7, in his agonizing description of not doing what he wants but doing the very things he hates, of wanting to do what is right but not being able to do it, Paul describes not the experience of life in the Spirit but life under the reign of sin and death. In fact, the Spirit is not mentioned in chapter 7 at all. This is life apart from the Spirit. Paul identifies with his readers who have suffered under the terrorizing reign of the old order. But Christ has rescued his children from the body of death so that, in spite of their sins, there is no condemnation for them. As the new order is breaking in, they are empowered to live by the Spirit rather than continuing to be controlled by the law of sin and death (7:24-8:2).

BAPTISM AND THE BIRTH OF THE NEW AGE

Now we are in a position to see how Paul's discussion of baptism in chapter 6 fits into the whole. If Christ rescued them while they were sinners and the very enemies of God (5:6-11), if under the old regime of Adam sin increased but under the reign of Christ grace has abounded all the more (5:20), then they should live as baptized people, grasped by the new order, turning their backs to the old. Just because grace increases as sin increases doesn't mean that how they live doesn't matter. It matters greatly. Their baptism does not open the door for them to participate in greater sin even though grace would abundantly cover it. Rather, baptism empowers them to reject sin because, in Christ, they died to it. Their baptism has ushered them into the power of the new order. In other words, they do not have to live under the power of sin described in Romans 7 but can live as adopted children under the power of the Spirit, citizens of the new age described in Romans 8. Christ's death, which they experienced in their baptism, has freed them from slavery to the old ways. They are dead to sin; therefore, they must not let sin rule over them. They are under grace, so they should live like it (6:1-14).

Further, Paul tells them that they will be slaves to something, either sin that leads to death or obedience that leads to righteousness. So he asks them, what was the advantage you gained under the old order, under the reign of sin? All you got was death. What, then, is the advantage you gain under the new order, under the reign of righteousness? The advantage you get is sanctification (6:19, 22). In other words, you are made holy.

Here it is, then. Here is the point we have been driving toward all along. Baptism is not a legal transaction in heaven or the cause for a transfer of spiritual funds in God's eternal accounting system. Rather, in baptism we died to a way of living that is passing away in the old order of things. In baptism we have hitched our lives to the power of the new age ushered in by the death of Christ. In baptism, Christ not only makes us members of his church, he not only forgives our past sins, but he empowers us to live holy lives today. To be holy is to live differently, not sharing in the spirit of the old order. To be holy is to live eschatologically, that is, to live as children of the new age even though we see evidence of the old one everywhere around us.

Since the death and resurrection of Christ, we have been living between the ages. We understand something of both the "now" and the "not yet" of God's kingdom. While we are blessed with a foretaste of the new order, we still live under the effects of the old. For modern Christians this means at least three things. First, twenty centuries removed from the message of Paul, we are still living in the labor pains of the new age. I have never given birth to a child, of course, but I have been very near at the birth of three. I can testify to what every husband who watches his wife give birth knows: this is hard, often painful work. We in the church are participants in the labor and delivery of the new age. In this case, however, we are not the parents but the offspring. We live in days when the church is experiencing a measure of pain. We should not be surprised, even when some of the pain is self-inflicted.

Second, these are serious times. Much is at stake. We had better know what is worth our time and attention. We can't afford to squander our current opportunities by expending our energies on things that don't ultimately matter. And we had better be clear what things matter and what don't.

Third, when Christians are contentious and divisive, when we speak unkindly toward others, we see clear evidence that the old order has not yet passed away, even among us. In our fragmentation, we reveal signs of the old age of sin and death. In those moments, we pray fervently for the full inbreaking of the kingdom of God. At the same time we give thanks that in baptism the oil of God's anointing has broken over us so that we live forgiven and holy within God's kingdom even here and now.

Do Not Think You Are Wiser Than You Are

In these first eight chapters, Paul has laid a remarkable foundation, not only in calling the Gentiles to an awareness of their indebtedness to the Jews, not only in leveling the ground between them by reminding them of the sin in which they have equally shared, but also in calling them to holy living based on the righteousness of God that they all received. Now he can speak candidly to the very real problems they face, to the hostility that threatens to undermine their mission and future.

As modern readers we must not sanitize the conflict in the Roman church or any of the other churches in the ancient world.

Those who argue that early Christians experienced no diversity, that Christian unity means doing and believing everything alike, simply have not grasped the tensions that lay at the heart of virtually every epistle in the New Testament. What caused these letters to be written were not small disagreements or incidental problems. While they shared a common faith and a common commitment to the lordship of Christ, early Christians did things differently. They believed and practiced many different things. Unity was not a matter of aligning all of their beliefs. It was about Christ transforming them into a united community in spite of their differences. That was certainly the case in the Roman church.

While abstaining from meat and keeping holy days seem like small issues to contemporary Christians, they mattered a great deal to many in the ancient world. They mattered as much as many of the things that divide modern churches today. These beliefs and practices were more than traditions; they were the very identity of a substantial number of early Christians. It was difficult enough for Jewish Christians to be expelled from Rome by the emperor, returning five years later to see their churches moved from synagogues to homes and led by Gentiles. But it was intolerable for them to see how these churches were being run. Many of their old practices had been eliminated. New behaviors, Gentile behaviors, had become the norm. Church was not the way they remembered it or the way they wanted it. It was not surprising that some of them formed their own assemblies in other homes with people they knew, people who were like them.

For Gentile Christians, the return of the Jews had created equally great difficulties. Like a cranky old uncle who had moved unexpectedly into the family home, the returning Jewish Christians disrupted what the Gentile Christians had become comfortable with. The Jews insisted on behavior that had nothing to do with the gospel, the Gentiles thought. So they wanted to meet by themselves in their own homes? Good riddance. Let everyone go their own way.

Within this tinderbox Paul writes. Listen to his heart as he pleads with them, beginning with the closing verses of Romans 11.

Dear Romans, don't claim to be wiser than you are. God is in charge, not you. God does what God will do. He can justify us all in spite of our sin. He can graft Gentiles onto the Jewish vine. He can do to the people of Israel whatever he chooses. God is responsible for everything he does. May his character and work be praised. His judgments are unsearchable. We will never figure it all out.

Therefore, because you have received the righteousness of God, because he has transferred you by the power of the cross from the old order to the new, I urge you to lay your lives down on the altar of sacrifice for his sake. I beg you not to be conformed to the values and practices of the current age but to be transformed into a new way of thinking and living shaped by the cross.

Don't congratulate yourselves about who you are, what you know, or what you do. You are a part of a body of believers that is larger than you. It doesn't belong to you. It is the one body of Christ. God has given you all different gifts. Your task is to use those gifts proportionately to the grace given to you, which is to say, fully and deeply, not for your own sake but for the sake of the others. You are not just individual members of Christ's church; you are members of one another. Live like it!

When Paul urges his readers not to be conformed to the values of the world but to be transformed by the renewing of their minds, he is not being theoretical. "Present your bodies as living sacrifices" is not just vivid prose worthy of memorization. Rather, Paul is trying to affect how Roman Christians treat one another every day, especially in the context of substantial differences. His language becomes specific and personal. He continues in 12:9:

Don't just pretend to love each other. Even with the profound differences that you are all aware of, love each other authentically. Go overboard in honoring everyone else without concern that you will be honored in return. Give generously to everyone who needs it. And when strangers come into your midst, people who are not like you, receive them into your homes. Serve them. Eat with them. Honor them.

Live in harmony even with those you disagree with. Spend time with people you find difficult. As I said before, do not think you are wiser than you are. You don't have it all figured out. If someone treats you badly, be kind in return. Choose to be people of peace no matter what anyone else says or does. If others mistreat you, your responsibility is not to get back at them. God sees the big picture. He will deal with them as he chooses. Your job is to serve them and to respond to their evil with your good.

You are experiencing the devastating effects of governmental intervention into your affairs. The mission of the church is at stake. Do everything you can to live obediently. Pay your taxes. Honor the authorities.

Let me tell you again, love one another. This is no small matter. You know what time it is. You know that we stand perched between the ages. Wake up! The night is gone. The new day is dawning. In your baptism, you took off the old clothes, the behaviors that reflect the old age. You put aside the desire to indulge yourselves. You turned your back to drunkenness, frivolousness, bickering, and jealousy. You put on new clothes. You walked away from darkness and into the light. You put on the Lord Jesus Christ!

Beginning in 14:1 Paul addresses the dietary practices and related issues that were polarizing the church. Note whom he calls weak.

Welcome the person who is weak in the faith. You who know that Christianity does not depend on keeping certain dietary rules, receive those who are weak, who still live by them. Those who eat and drink freely don't condemn those who do not. And those of you whose very identity is at stake in abstaining from certain foods and drink, you who continue to keep the Jewish traditions, don't judge those who practice otherwise. Don't you know that God himself has welcomed them? God has embraced these Gentiles, not on your terms but on his. Who do you think you are, passing judgment on them? They are not accountable to you. They stand or fall before the Lord. And let me be clear: he will hold them up because he is able to make them stand.

Some of you observe certain days as holy. Others of you see every day the same. If you observe holy days, do so in honor of the Lord. Those of you who choose to ignore Jewish dietary restrictions, eat in honor of the Lord. Those of you who keep the dietary regimen, abstain from those foods in honor of the Lord. Whatever you do, give thanks to God, every one of you. This is about him, not about any of us. We don't live to ourselves; we live to the Lord. We don't die to ourselves; we die to the Lord. Either way, we are the Lord's. Since that is the case, why do you spend your time condemning each other? Why do you hate your brother or sister? All of us stand before God. We are accountable to him.

Therefore, stop passing judgment on one another. At the same time, don't place obstacles in each other's way. I know very well that no food is unclean in and of itself, but for those who believe certain foods are unclean, they are unclean for them. It's one thing for someone not to like it when you eat certain foods. It's another for your eating and drinking to injure them. People can live together with differences. But you must not let what you eat cause someone else's ruin. That's a different matter altogether. If by your eating and drinking you cause others to fall, if your practices encourage those who believe these things are wrong to participate in them anyway, then both of you are wrong. Understand this clearly: the kingdom of God is not about eating and drinking but about righteousness and peace and joy in the Holy Spirit. So whatever you do, aggressively pursue peace with others. Do not, because of your beliefs and practices about food, destroy the work of God.

Those of you who are strong, who understand and enjoy your freedom to eat and drink, put up with those who do not. Seek to please the others in the same way that Christ sought

> to please you. I know that this is difficult. I know the problems
> are real and the tension is high. But may God grant you the
> ability, in accordance with Christ Jesus, to live in harmony
> with one another in spite of your differences so that you may
> praise God not separately but with one voice. So I tell you
> again, welcome one another in the same way that Christ has
> welcomed you, for the glory of God.

Paul writes to a church that contains many friends and fellow
workers from across the empire, a church dear to him and pivotal to
the expansion of Christianity westward. The substantial differences
among them, however, have created a clear threat to their future.
They needed more than just a reduction of tension; they needed to
be a people of welcome.

Every church I know experiences tensions of some sort. Most are
the little frictions that arise when human wills rub against each
other. They come from a careless word, a perceived slight, a mis-
interpreted motive. They occur when we are tired or stressed, when
we are shortsighted or distracted, when we speak too quickly or perhaps not at all. They are part of being a family. Most of us hardly
notice. We understand that relationships are hard. Over time, with a
hug or a word of encouragement, we address the differences, extend
grace, and church life goes on.

Sometimes, however, these tensions grow into something more
substantial. Pettiness festers into condemnation. Silence hardens
into distance. Disagreement becomes accusation. Now sin has its
opening. The church's work is hobbled, and discouragement pene-
trates the community like a slow-acting toxin. At worst, hard feelings produce the seeds of anger and resentment that, when planted
and nurtured, bear the fruit of division. Then the church is paralyzed, its ministries handcuffed, its mission derailed.

Often the differences are of a personal nature. People can't get
along. Individuals abuse power. Someone gets hurt. At other times
the differences grow out of cultural expectations. People get used to
doing things in certain ways and then confuse their traditional practices and rituals with the gospel. Sometimes the differences are about

doctrine. People sincerely disagree about the meaning of Scripture. They dig in their heels, not to be obstinate, but because they want to be faithful to God and are not willing to compromise what they believe to be the truth.

Romans speaks a powerful word into such situations. Our contemporary problems are too similar to what the Roman Christians experienced to overlook Paul's clear message. I think he would say at least two things to us.

Passing Judgment

First, we must stop judging, however strongly we might disagree with one another. All of us stand before God as sinners. None of us has reason to boast in who we are or what we know. The righteousness of God has been revealed to us all, even in our sin. We are in relationship to him on the basis of what he has done, not what we have done. We are the recipients of his mercy, which we have received in faith.

If all of us stand before God as sinners, if all of us have received his mercy, then we view each other differently. We do not condemn those who share in our own sinful nature, those for whom Christ died. We understand the difference between our task and God's. He is the one who bestows righteousness. He does the reckoning. He is judge of all. We all stand before him. We are sinners in need of God's grace; therefore, we see each other with compassion and tenderness.

We are not being asked to abandon what we believe any more than Paul was asking the Jewish Christians to abandon their dietary practices or asking the Gentile Christians to alter their beliefs. We should study hard and think deeply. We should express our faith and not casually surrender what we believe. But we must not assume that we are wiser than we are. For the sake of Christ, we must be willing to live with differences, even profound ones.

Let me be specific. It is easy to talk about differences if they are hypothetical or if they come from a distant past or if they don't matter much. Among Churches of Christ, it is relatively easy today to talk about differences over musical notations in songbooks, a hot topic in the middle of the nineteenth century, or over pacifism, which divided churches around World War I. It isn't too painful to talk about the indwelling of the Holy Spirit, which was a topic of great debate during the 1960s and 70s when I was a young man. Handclapping and contemporary music are topics of more common conversation these days, but while most people have their preferences about them, they are generally not causes of division. None of them come close to the painful disputes between Jews and Gentiles in the early church. So let's take a deep breath and look at something closer to where at least some churches actually live.

Though the use of instrumental music was a dividing issue within the Restoration Movement a hundred years ago, it continues to be a topic of considerable importance in the early years of the twenty-first century. To most of us in Churches of Christ, it is a matter of identity. A cappella singing is not just what we do but who we are.

Many within this fellowship believe that singing without instruments in the assembly is more than a tradition. It is God's will. Out of their study, because of their understanding of texts in Ephesians and Colossians, among other passages, because they believe that the silence of the New Testament on musical instruments prohibits their use, and because of the near universal agreement of historians that early Christian assemblies did not include instruments of music in worship, some believe strongly that they must not be used in churches today. These are noble arguments coming from godly people who are trying to be faithful to Scripture and obedient to God.

Others within Churches of Christ do not buy these conclusions at all. While no one believes we must use musical instruments, many believe we at least can. Some insist that the passages in Ephesians and Colossians could not have been condemning a practice that did not even appear in the church for almost a thousand years. They believe the Bible is silent about many practices that are common in our churches today. A few argue that employing musical instruments in worship is not only permissible by God but may, in fact, be desirable in order to connect with the surrounding culture. Those who express these beliefs do so out of a deep love of God, a commitment to Scripture, and a desire to be obedient to him.

In reality, there is at least a third group that does not believe that a cappella singing is required by God but advocates the practice not only out of the strength of the tradition but out of a theology of full congregational participation, that it is the best if not the only way for the church to worship. Clearly, whatever one's position, this is a volatile issue about which many people are passionate. Perhaps for Churches of Christ it comes close to the kind of dispute evident in the Roman church. Here is an opportunity for the gospel. Here is where the doctrine of unity comes into play. People should study, think, and speak about such a topic. Christians may feel strongly about their position and may not understand how anyone could believe differently. But over this issue the church must not divide. Rather, as Paul urged the Roman Christians in a remarkably similar context, we should welcome one another, even in our differences, for the glory of God.

Similarly, many Christians believe that the weight of Scripture moves inexorably toward greater inclusion of women in leadership in Christian assemblies. They are not willing to sell out the gospel in order to accommodate contemporary culture, but they believe the preponderance of biblical texts supports such inclusion and that the few passages of exclusion describe aberrations not common in our churches today, such as the disorder created by certain women in Corinth who were questioning some with the gift of prophesy, thus disrupting the assembly (1 Cor. 14:26-40), and the divisiveness of particular women in Ephesus who were domineering in their behavior and who perpetuated false teaching (1 Tim. 2:9-15; 5:11-16). Most who hold these positions do not in any way reject the teaching of Scripture but believe in its full authority. They are trying sincerely to serve God and desire to be obedient to him.

Others are appalled at such positions. They believe the passages of exclusion are so clear, so specific, that they can hardly be misunderstood: women are to keep silent; they are not to have authority over men or teach men. Those who hold this position teach that male spiritual leadership has always been God's will and that worship assemblies in which women function in public roles are inappropriate and unacceptable. Those who advocate this view do so out

of sincere hearts, out of a commitment to Scripture, and out of an
earnest desire to please God.

Both positions are based on an understanding of God's will.
Both reflect a commitment to be obedient to him. Both grow out of
sincere hearts and diligent study. Loving and encouraging one
another in the midst of such differences will be difficult, but over
such an issue the church must not divide.

So now we have decisions to make. Some of those decisions
have to do with what we practice in our own local congregations.
But the greater decisions, perhaps, have to do with how we treat one
another. Now Paul's letter to the Romans has direct bearing on us.
Will we despise those with whom we differ? Will we condemn them?
Will we excoriate their character or challenge their belief in Scripture?
Will we call them cowards or heretics? Will we marginalize them in
our congregations or pressure them to leave? Will we be relieved when
they find a church across town that is filled with people more like
them? Can we even talk together? Can we sit down together to pray?

Different congregations will make different choices regarding
these and other issues, each one working with its own members in
prayer and study in order to be obedient to God, trying to serve him
faithfully. Will we claim as brothers and sisters only those who
believe and practice the way we do? In too many places, churches
are lining up against churches, preachers against preachers, schools
against schools. Some church leaders and Christian journals are
openly calling for division. They do so because they believe they are
being conservative, out of a belief that division in such circumstances is what God wants. I am often appalled that a direct appeal
to Scripture for the cause of Christian unity, such as the one I am
making here, is labeled liberal or heretical.

Why do you pass judgment on your brothers and sisters, Paul
asks Roman Christians in the midst of tense conflict. Why do you
despise them? Why do you condemn those whom the Lord makes
stand? Why would you allow your behavior to cause the ruin of one
for whom Christ died? The kingdom of God is not about these divisive issues, however strongly we may feel about them. Rather the
kingdom of God is about righteousness and peace and joy in the

Holy Spirit. May the God of steadfastness and encouragement grant that we might live in harmony with one another, in accordance with Christ Jesus, so that together we might with one voice glorify the God and Father of our Lord Jesus Christ.

A SANCTUARY OF WELCOME

Second, Paul calls us not only to stop judging others but also to engage in a ministry of active hospitality. Welcome each other, he tells the Romans. Welcome those who are weak in the faith. Extend hospitality even to strangers. Welcome one another just as Christ welcomed you. Greet one another. Greet Priscilla and Aquila, who work with me in Christ Jesus. Greet the church in their house. Greet my beloved Epaenetus, who was the first convert in Asia for Christ. Greet all the saints. Greet one another with a holy kiss. All the churches of Christ with whom I now minister and worship greet you.

This sort of hospitality is far beyond a smiling greeter handing out welcome cards to visitors in the church foyer. It is more than a sleepy opening greeting in a morning worship service extending "a warm welcome to all our visitors." It's certainly more than a caffé latté at Starbucks or a chicken salad at the corner restaurant with our closest friends. Fellowship that extends only to people like ourselves is hardly the radical Christian fellowship to which we are called.

Paul insists that his readers receive one another. Strangers should be invited into our homes. People with whom we disagree should be welcomed to our tables. How many disputes would be addressed more constructively if we spent less time at the water cooler talking about people and more time in the living room talking with them? How many churches would continue the practice of virtual racial segregation if it were our regular practice to welcome people of different ethnic and social backgrounds into our homes? Paul repeatedly calls his readers to active, aggressive hospitality. Welcome one another. Why? Because Christ welcomed you.

We have been baptized into Christ. We participate in his suffering. We share his brokenness. In our baptism we publicly declare our sinfulness, and God covers us by his righteousness. Through it our sins are forgiven, our hearts washed clean. But our baptism not only saves us, it also thrusts us into relationship with other broken people. It empowers us for holy living. It removes the scales of judgment from our souls. It opens our arms to receive others, to greet with warmth and sincere love even those who oppose us.

In baptism we have died to the old order, to a way of living that is passing away. We have been captured by the power of the new age ushered in by the death of Christ. All around us the old order seems to be thriving. Sin seems unchecked and even celebrated. We are tempted in every way to live by the old values, to treat one another by the old standards. Wake up! The night is gone. The new day is dawning. In your baptism, you took off the old clothes, the behaviors that reflect the old age. You put aside bickering, gossip, judgment, and jealousy. You put on new clothes. You walked away from darkness and into the light. You put on the Lord Jesus Christ. He has empowered you to live like it.

Baptism transforms our eyes so that we see one another differently. It transforms our hearts so that we reach out to others in compassion. It transforms our homes into centers of hospitality. It transforms our churches into sanctuaries of welcome. Restoring baptism to its place at the center of things, not only concerning whether we are saved but how we live, will be our greatest hope. Here in baptism a broken people will meet a broken Christ. Here in the water the resurrected Christ will make us his glorious people. Here among the baptized community we will become a people of peace, and our churches will become safe places. Here, when we embrace fully our baptism, we will become a people of hope, a people of compassion, a people of mercy and holiness.

GREET ONE ANOTHER

For years I have played to my preaching classes a tape of a sermon by Fred Craddock on Romans 16. Though one might not expect a compelling sermon from the list of names Paul includes in this final chapter, and though I have heard it over a dozen times, I have never listened to it without tears. His concluding story speaks eloquently to the power of baptism and the call to holy living.[3]

Before I married and served in the little mission in the Appalachians, I moved down to a place on Watts Bar Lake, between Chattanooga and Knoxville, a little village. My church immerses, and it was held, this baptismal service, on Easter evening at sundown. Now out on the sandbar, I, with the candidates for baptism, moved into the water, and then they moved across to the shore where the little congregation was gathered, singing around a fire and cooking supper. They had constructed little booths for changing clothes with hanging blankets. As the candidates moved from the water, they went in, changed clothes and went to the fire in the center. Finally, last of all, I went over, changed clothes, and went to the fire.

Once we were all around the fire, this was the ritual of that tradition. Glenn Hickey, always Glenn, introduced the new people, gave their names, where they lived, and their work. Then the rest of us formed a circle around them, while they stayed warm at the fire. The ritual was that each person in the circle then gave her or his name, and said this, "My name is..., and if you ever need somebody to do washing and ironing...." "My name is....If you ever need anybody to chop wood...." "My name is....If you ever need anybody to babysit...." "My name is....If you ever need anybody to repair your house...." "My name is....If you ever need anybody to sit with the sick...." "My name is..., and if you ever need a car to go to town...." and around the circle.

Then we ate, and we had a square dance. And then at a time they knew, I didn't know, Percy Miller, with thumbs in his bibbed overalls, would stand up and say, "Time to go," and everybody left. He lingered behind and, with his big shoe, kicked sand over the dying fire. And my first experience of that, he saw me standing there still, and he looked at me and said, "Craddock, folks don't ever get any closer than this."

In that little community, they have a name for that. I've heard it in other communities too. In that community, their name for that is "church." They call that "church."

NOTES

1. For example, Priscilla and Aquila had a church meeting in their house (16:5). A group met with Asyncritus, Phlegon, Hermes, Patrobas, and Hermas (16:14), and another met with Philologus, Julia, Nereus, and Olympas (16:15). Moreover, it is possible that the "family of Aristobulus" (16:10) and the "family of Narcissus" (16:11) refer to house churches. Other names are grouped together in ways that might also indicate regular association in house churches.

2. Gal. 2:10; 1 Cor. 16:1-4; 2 Cor. 8-9.

3. This and other great stories from Fred Craddock sermons can be found in *Craddock Stories*, edited by my friend Mike Graves with Richard Ward (St. Louis: Chalice Press, 2001). This story can be found on page 151.

CHAPTER SIX

COMING TOGETHER PEACEMEAL

The Table of Reconciliation and Grace

> *I think that the Church is the only thing that is going to*
> *make the terrible world we are coming to endurable; the only*
> *thing that makes the Church endurable is that it is somehow*
> *the body of Christ and that on this we are fed.*
>
> —Flannery O'Connor

A sense of dread began to settle over my shoulders, filling my lungs, and finally seeping deep into bone marrow. I was almost thirteen, and my parents had just spoken two words that send fear into any child's heart: "family reunion."

I recalled having been to one of those vile events when I was little. I didn't remember much about it except that a lot of old people that I had never met kept coming over to me and clucking. "He is just precious." "Do you know who I am? Do you? Why, I'm your Aunt Novalee." Even as a little boy I knew my parents' brothers and sisters, and I knew this woman named Novalee wasn't one of them. Who were these people, and why were they posing as my aunts? "You look just like your grandfather." That sent chills down my back as I glanced at Papa's largish ears and uni-brow. "You have gotten so big," they lied. I was just about the smallest boy in my school. My head was patted. My hair was tussled. They were everywhere, these old people, smelling of beauty shop and sweat.

I had promised myself, as much as a little boy can promise anything, that I would never again participate in such a grisly affair. There was little I could do, however, when Mom announced, "We are going to have a family reunion this summer...here at our house."

We spent long, hard weeks preparing the place. Our family home is in the country, just outside of Abilene. My two brothers and I mowed what seemed like several hectares of grass and weeds. We moved large rocks and sawed off the dead branches of several mesquite trees. We painted the trim of the house, planted flowers, and patched the gravel driveway just in case the once-in-a-century July rain occurred on the day of the big event.

This was a reunion of my mom's family, the Muns clan. Papa, my grandfather, was the oldest of his siblings. His generation of Munses were not the most prolific child bearers, at least compared to many who had begun families in the early years of the twentieth century, so I was never quite sure where all of these people came from. Perhaps a hundred men, women, and children were present that day, including the wife of my mother's cousin, "Aunt" Novalee. As soon as some of the kids arrived, we raced down the bluff to the pond, or as we call it in West Texas, the tank. Soon the air was filled with the whine of spinning reels and the shrieks of children catching sun perch.

Before long Mama, my grandmother, came down the hill wearing a long dress and an apron. Someone handed her a bamboo pole. We watched with awe and admiration as this strong, thin woman in her seventies blithely maneuvered the worm onto the hook and swung the cork and sinker near the deepest part of the tank. Within a few seconds, her cork darted into the water. She pulled with all her might. The large catfish swung over her head and onto the bank where it slipped off the hook and began flopping toward the water and freedom. Mama positioned herself between the fish and the destination it so desperately sought, scooping it into her apron while everyone cheered.

Shortly after noon we heard shouts from the top of the hill telling us to come quickly and wash our hands. It was time to eat. Under the mesquite trees, tables had been set up and covered with white linen cloths and an assortment of large pottery dishes. What was in those dishes, of course, was what drew the kids into the middle of the family circle: mountains of crispy fried chicken, slabs of roast beef standing in pools of natural gravy, mounds of mashed potatoes with real butter slithering down the slopes, green beans saturated with bacon drippings, corn, squash, cabbage, tomatoes, cucumbers and onions soaked in vinegar, deviled eggs, boiled baby okra, a couple of casseroles covered with little fried onion ringlets, Mama's world famous chow chow, homemade rolls and cornbread, pecan pie, snickerdoodle cookies, and the *pièce de résistance*—freshly baked peach cobbler. Mama caught my eye and glanced at the corner of one of the tables to a small dish that contained a little vice that the two of us shared, jalapeño peppers from her garden. She winked.

Papa led the prayer. As the "thees" and "thous" rolled off his tongue, I peeked at my cousins who, like me, were caught with their eyes open. We grinned and bowed our heads again. For the rest of the afternoon we ate. Before some of us had even taken our first bite of potatoes, the old folks started telling stories. They talked about growing up in Lorraine, a little town fifty miles or so to the west, about hard life and family joys. They spoke of people they had known, of singing hymns at the old church, of hunting wolves and playing baseball. Uncle Harvey, Papa's brother, who was about 6' 6" and had a rifle for an arm, regaled us with stories about being a pitcher in the minor leagues and how he had almost made it to the Big Show. Their youngest brother, Ottis, told stories about a year some time after he turned seventy in which he had purchased a bus pass from Greyhound and traveled across the country. Aunt Ola chattered about staying up all night cooking her cabbage. We cousins whispered to each other stories about our adventures in Papa's lumberyard in Sweetwater and, on simmering hot days, walking into the cool refrigerated rooms at the flower shop where Mama worked.

After cobbler and ice cream and a short game of "burn out" with Uncle Harvey, who could still throw a baseball two hundred miles an hour, the families began to gather the folding chairs, card tables, and leftovers, packing them into the cars for their journeys home. My family spent the rest of the evening cleaning up. When I fell into bed about midnight, I felt a contentment deeper than I had ever known. I was not the same boy as the one who had awakened that morning. After sitting at table with the kinfolks, after pulling wishbones with great aunts and patting the heads of the littlest cousins, after listening to the stories of my family and my past, I knew who I was. When you know that, nothing is ever the same again.

It wasn't just the gathering of people, of course. It was the stories. And it was the food. I cannot imagine the same thing happening if we had just gone down to the local civic auditorium, each of us standing at the podium in turn, introducing ourselves and telling an anecdote or two. At the table we ate and laughed, we teased and reminisced. The food provided more than physical sustenance: it lubricated conversations, tore down barriers of age and position, pushed aside our distractions and ameliorated our worries, and bound us together in profound and mysterious ways. To eat and drink together is to participate in God's creation with immediacy and delight. It is to receive and enjoy God's generous gifts. Every meal, for those who can see it, is an experience of grace.

To Eat and Drink with God

Good food and good company are inextricably linked. In fact, the word "company" comes from two Latin words meaning "sharing bread together." Companionship is more than people sitting and talking to each other. To have company in one's home assumes the host family extends hospitality, and hospitality can hardly be imagined apart from food. No fancy setting is required, no expensive sit-down meal. Just a cup of coffee or a glass of iced tea will do, chips and salsa perhaps, or cookies and milk. It is one thing to conduct a meeting, taking care of assigned tasks, formulating plans, and making decisions. It's another thing altogether to visit over food and drink. Even in modern Western cultures, which are so oriented around tasks and time, to receive someone without offering something to eat or drink would be rude. In most other cultures, it would be a serious insult.

Eating together is a sign of friendship, of relationship, of community. It marks important events and draws strangers together. At a wedding, however large or small, the family of the bride invites all the wedding guests to a reception following the ceremony. There the two families and all the guests mingle, not just "friends of the bride" or "friends of the groom," but friends and family of the new couple. There they eat and drink, laugh and talk, and throw flowers and intimate things. And a few years later, when the couple's children send invitations to all their parents' friends to join them in celebrating the fiftieth anniversary of that wedding, they make sure there is plenty of food for all the guests. How else could such an important event be celebrated apart from eating and drinking together? That's what communities do. In many ways, that's how communities are formed. Eating bread creates company. Sitting at table establishes relationship.

Moreover, in many cultures, both modern and ancient, eating a meal is a sign of protection and the cessation of hostilities. William Willimon tells a story about a nomad being pursued across the desert by his foes. The desperate man comes upon an encampment. He rushes up to the tents, hoping that these strangers will receive him. He throws back the curtains of the head tent. The inhabitants have just begun to eat. Breathlessly he looks into their faces. Will they receive him or turn him away? They motion for him to enter and be seated. He breathes a sigh of relief. His pursuers finally reach the camp. They go to the tent he has entered. They also throw back the curtains, ready to seize the man and kill him. But when they see him seated at the table, they draw back and leave him in peace, for it is a great act of hostility toward the host to trouble a person who is seated at someone's table.[1]

And so it is with us. "The Lord is my shepherd, I shall not be in want," says the psalmist. "Even though I walk through the valley of the shadow of death, I will not be afraid of evil, because you are with me." "In the presence of my enemies, you prepare for me a table." We race into the encampment out of breath from our desperate run. We throw back the curtains of the tent. There stands God before a sprawling feast. He gestures to a place he has been holding for us in the midst of his family. What is happening outside the tent is no longer our concern. We have been welcomed to the banquet of God.

Perhaps the most remarkable meal described in the Old Testament occurs in Exodus 24. In the wilderness near Mt. Horeb, Moses told the people all of Yahweh's words and laws. They responded, "We will do everything the LORD has said." Moses took blood from young bulls that had been sacrificed. Half he put on the altar; the rest he poured into basins. Holding the basins, he turned to the people and said, "This is the blood of the covenant that the LORD has made with you." He splashed the blood upon the people. Then Moses and Aaron, Nadab and Abihu, and the seventy elders of Israel went up to the mountain where the God of Israel awaited them. Under his feet was something like a pavement of sapphire, clear as the sky. They saw God, and they ate and drank.

What extraordinary words! God shared with them his heart. He gave them his torah, his way. They heard, and they agreed to keep his law. Thus the elders sat down with God and sealed the deal. They ratified the covenant. God welcomed them to his mountain, and God ate and drank with them.

This meal was an important part of Israel's memory. Each time they recalled the story, they were drawn back to their wedding day with God, to the establishment of their covenant with him, to the extraordinary feast at which God sat down at table with them. But it also fueled their imaginations about what God would do in the future. Isaiah spoke of a time that God would gather his people again for a great banquet. On the eve of God's destruction of Jerusalem, Isaiah tells them of a time when they will gather again around the mountain.

> On this mountain the LORD Almighty will prepare
> > a feast of rich food for all peoples,
> a banquet of aged wine—
> > the best of meats and the finest of wines.
> On this mountain he will destroy
> > the shroud that enfolds all peoples,
> the sheet that covers all nations;
> > he will swallow up death forever.   (Isaiah 25:6-7)

God has prepared a time, says Isaiah, when he will gather his people around him again, but this time it will not be just the elders but all the people. It will not only be the chosen people, the descendents of Abraham, but God will invite to this table all the nations of the earth. He will serve them the best meat and the finest wines. And God will eat with them there. And in their presence he will eat death itself. He will grasp death with both hands, chew it, and swallow it. It will be a fine banquet indeed.

As this story was retold in Jewish communities in later years, however, the point became distorted. The people of God could not envision all the nations gathered at that great meal with God, only Israel. The Essene community, contemporary with John the Baptist and Jesus, told the story that God would invite not all Jews but only perfect Jews to the banquet. No blind, no lame, no sinners would receive an invitation. But when Jesus tells the story in Luke 14, he says that, in the face of those who have received the master's invitation to the banquet but have declined with false and insulting excuses, he will invite the poor, the crippled, the blind and the lame. Then the master tells his servant to go out to the roads and country lanes, out where the Gentiles are, and compel them to come in so that they also might enjoy the great feast. All the barriers will be torn down. Everything that divides, that marks some as less worthy or desirable, will be taken away. And the host will eat with his guests.

Sometime later, at Jesus' supper with his disciples in the upper room, Jesus takes the cup and blesses it, saying, "This cup is the new covenant in my blood." Though the memories of Passovers past and God's deliverance of his people from slavery are the dominant images of this gathering, Jesus also connects it to another meal. At Mt. Horeb Moses sprinkled blood on the people saying, "This is the blood of the covenant." There at the mountain, with all the elders of Israel, over food and drink, God sealed his promise. Only later will Jesus' disciples fully grasp that as they ate the bread and drank the wine with their Lord, they were also eating and drinking with God.

A WORD, A KISS, AND A MEAL

Only a short while after Jesus sat at table with his disciples, churches all over the empire gathered together to eat and drink. This was an indispensable part of the believers' life in community. One could hardly imagine being a disciple of Jesus during those early years apart from eating meals with other believers. Their meals did not merely reflect that a community had been formed but functioned to form the community itself. Slaves and masters sat next to each other. Jews and Gentiles ate together. Men and women shared their food and their faith. Doing this every week, over time, changes people. And so the Christians gathered to receive the Word and share bread and wine, to offer prayers and take care of those who were in need.

They have come together this night after sundown on the day the Romans called the Day of the Sun, the day when believers proclaimed their Lord was raised from the dead. They have slipped quietly through narrow streets and market stalls, through the alleys and courtyards of the city. Here is an old Jewish couple, there a Roman soldier. A father and mother guide their children through unfamiliar streets, helped by his parents as well the wife's unmarried sister and an orphaned teenaged boy who are part of the household. A married woman winds her way through the streets, nervous about being alone, concerned about her children, anxious because her pagan husband did not want her to come. Two slaves walk silently together toward the meeting place, old friends who have suffered much. They are grateful for the late hour that allows them the opportunity to come for worship. They are met at the doorway of a modest home by a minor city official and his wife who extend welcome to all.

The house is filled with the noise of family gathered, of people wildly dissimilar who call each other brother and sister. They tell stories about their week, about small victories and more than a little suffering. They are quickly aware of who is not present. They pay special attention to any strangers who have found their way to this gathering of disciples.

In the dim light of the oil lamps, a plain wooden table is visible in the middle of the room. Some are seated and others stand around the edge. The house falls silent as a man begins to read with a clear, firm voice. He is an elder of the community, wise and respected. He is seated in the *kathedra*, the teacher's chair at the head of the table. He reads from Scripture, from the Greek translation of the Hebrew Bible, whose pictures of the steadfast love of God have shaped them in substantial ways. He shares a letter that has been copied and passed along from a church in a nearby town. He takes his time. When he finishes, he carefully sets down the scrolls. In a brief discourse he urges the believers to go and do the things they have heard.

A cantor leads them in prayers and hymns from the Psalter, the gathered Christians responding phrase by phrase. Then they all rise. With their eyes open and hands lifted, they begin to pray one by one. They offer their petitions to God, pleading for his help and thanking him for his mercies. One woman's relative was recently arrested. One man's slave has run away, and he has no one to help with the harvest. Across the room someone offers a prayer for a servant he knows who has been badly beaten. Some have been shunned by neighbors. Others have lost jobs. One woman is expecting her first child. An old man with dim sight and a trembling voice urges God to grant courage to this household of faith.

When the prayers cease, the room erupts with the sounds of greeting. Everyone exchanges kisses, offering Christian affection to each person present. The kisses are mouth-to-mouth with persons of the same sex as well as the opposite sex, an expression of the remarkable intimacy of family. They extend to each other the peace of Christ.

Deacons (also called *ministri* or "servants") make their way through the gathered crowd, collecting loaves of bread and jugs of wine. The church's offering is laid on the table, each one having given bread and wine as a sign that they have also given of themselves. The bread is regular table bread. The wine is watered wine, the daily fare of household meals. This is ordinary food and drink. Nothing in the ingredients or the preparation makes them special. They are extraordinary because Christ is extraordinary, because of the profound significance of the body and blood of Christ to which they are connected, and because they are shared in faith with the assembled brothers and sisters.

One of the elders, with hands raised above the bread and wine, sends up thanksgiving to the Father of all saying, "We give thanks to you, our Father, for the Holy Vine of David, your child, which you made known to us through Jesus your child, to you be glory forever. We thank you for the life and knowledge that you made known to us. As this broken bread was scattered upon the mountains but was brought together and became one, so let your Church be gathered together from the ends of the earth into your kingdom, for yours is the glory and the power through Jesus Christ forever." He thus offers eucharist, or thanksgiving, for the bread and the wine. The prayer ends with the people singing out their assent, saying the "amen." By this covenant word the people publicly affirm the elder's thanksgiving and commit their lives again to the Lord, who has welcomed them to the table.

Each person is given a sizeable piece of the bread that has been blessed. Each one drinks from the large cup of wine that is passed among them. When all have eaten, the leftovers are collected by the deacons to be taken to those who are in need because of sickness or some other cause, to orphans and widows, to strangers who are passing through the city. After being fed by the Word, after extending and receiving the peace of Christ, after sharing together with Christ and one another at table, after offering prayers of thanksgiving and intercession, the worshippers slip into the streets and back to their homes, strengthened for what they will face, full of hope and courage.[2]

This picture is something like what early Christians experienced in their assemblies all across the first-century world. The gathering is almost shockingly intimate through the eyes of modern worshippers. Between the ministry of the word and the ministry of the table, at the hinge of the service, stood the kiss of peace. After hearing from God and before eating with him at the supper, Christians welcomed and received each other, encouraging one another and offering to one another the peace of Christ. Some of the pagans accused them of incest, of inappropriate familiarity with their "brothers" and "sisters." After a century or so, church leaders had to restrict the gesture to kisses on the cheek of people of the same sex. But in the early days of the church, this intimate kiss of peace reflected the depth of their relationship and their commitment to one another. Masters exchanged the peace of Christ with slaves, the wealthy with the poor, Gentiles with Jews, men with women, adults with children. Without sharing together in the peace of Christ, early Christians knew they would fail.

Living a godly life was hard. The followers of Jesus needed each other. They weren't strong enough alone. They weren't wise enough or courageous enough to sustain their faith without the support of their brothers and sisters. Church to them was not just a pleasant place to come each week, a gathering of friends and other nice folks, where they might dress themselves up, sing songs they liked, hear a nice sermon, pinch a wafer and sip a tiny cup of grape juice before heading back into their busy world. It was not the kind of gathering at which they would likely complain that the auditorium class had been moved, the sermon was too long, or a worship team was positioned up front. They came together because they knew by themselves they were in trouble. They needed someone to help strengthen their feeble arms and weak knees, someone to keep them from being discouraged. For this reason, the unity of the church was not a luxury, not a minor doctrine or marginal issue that could be ignored until everyone agreed on every issue. Each week, in the midst of their diversity, in spite of their differences, they exchanged with great intimacy the peace of Christ. Then they sat down together and ate and drank.

Such fellowship could hardly be faked. Unlike modern assemblies where many of us don't even know the names of the people with whom we are eating the Supper, where we can pretend to be loving and faithful and no one will know otherwise, Christians meeting in early house churches were bound together by necessity and by commitment. They were frequently ostracized by their neighbors because of their faith. Some were beaten or arrested. Many had friends who turned their backs on them, among both the Jewish and Gentile communities. That is why the breakdown of Christian unity within any group was devastating. And it is why divisions among Christians usually showed themselves first in their assemblies.

DINNER PARTIES AND CHURCH PARTIES

No church in the first century experienced more difficulty in creating or maintaining unity than the one in Corinth. It has stood for centuries as the patron saint of quarrels and division. By themselves the self-serving behaviors of many of its members were devastating, but when the whole church came together, the pathologies of the believers were especially destructive. Peace had been undermined in almost every way.

As we saw in Rome, and as was common throughout the empire in the first century, the Christians in Corinth apparently met regularly in homes. These homes served as places of service and hospitality, as centers of Christian fellowship and activity for those who were associated with them. From time to time, however, all of them gathered in one place (1 Cor. 11:18; 14:23), "the whole church" coming together to share the Supper and encourage one another. This was a different arrangement from what most modern churches experience. These were not self-contained local assemblies in the same city, the Northside Church and the Southside Church with independent programs and priorities. The house churches saw themselves as part of the same church. They helped and supported each other so that all were concerned about the entire community of believers. Moreover, Paul was able to address them as a single unit, as a "church" rather than "churches."[3]

Several prominent individuals, people of high social status, seemed to be generating most of the problems. Though Paul indicates that not many of his readers were "wise," "powerful," or "of noble birth" (1:26-28), obviously at least some of them were. In fact, the Corinthian church contained more than most. Among them were some governmental officials such as Erastus (Rom. 16:23) and other people of substantial enough wealth to have homes large enough for the groups to meet in. Moreover, while many of the Christians in Corinth were quite poor, many had enough resources that Paul could appeal to them regarding the Jerusalem collection (2 Cor. 8, 9). In a variety of ways, these wealthy citizens within the church in Corinth played a significant role in its internal problems.

When the whole church came together, the social distinctions became apparent. These assemblies were characterized not only by times of worship, including sharing the Lord's Supper together, but also by participating in full meals. These meals, or *agape* feasts as they were sometimes called, were not uncommon in the first century. But some of the Corinthian Christians modeled their behavior at these meals after the social conventions of their surrounding culture. Something resembling dinner clubs was popular among the upwardly mobile citizens of Corinth. These dinners provided opportunities for social networking as well as for personal pleasure. The feasts typically transitioned from a dinner banquet in which certain rules of etiquette were expected into drinking parties where only men were present and which often became displays of excess and immorality. At these social gatherings the more prominent individuals ate in the dining room of a home, the lower classes remaining in the atrium. Choice food and wine was served to the first group, the second having little or nothing.

Similar practices came to characterize the gatherings of the church. When Paul says that some went ahead with their own supper, one going hungry, another becoming drunk (11:21), they were reflecting the common practices of the pagans. The rich were having their fill and the poor were getting the leftovers. Moreover, as with the pagans, the meal itself was followed by a drinking party. Some elite Christians, after eating with their friends, began to drink heavily, while pushing aside the poor and slaves who waited in the atrium.

These Christians exhibited a "party spirit" in more than one sense. When Paul urges them to "wait for" one another (11:33), the word he uses is a common hospitality word. It might be that the well-to-do group started early and the poorer Christians arrived after everything had been eaten. More likely, however, Paul is telling them to wait on one another, that is, to serve one another at their common meal.

QUARRELS AND MORALS

Similar issues seem to be at stake in Paul's arguments in chapters 8-10 concerning meat offered to idols. Two things should be made clear. First, the issues in 1 Corinthians are different from those in Romans. The primary concerns in Romans 14-15 are about some who have scruples about eating meat and drinking wine. This is not the case in 1 Corinthians. In fact, the primary concern in Corinth was less about whether meat was eaten than where it was eaten. Moreover, there is no reference here to the "strong" as there is in Romans. Paul is not mediating between "strong" and "weak" Christians but between certain Corinthians and himself.

Second, Paul's discussion focuses on the behavior of primarily one group—some of the well-to-do Christians whose behavior reflected what was common among upscale Corinthians. To understand their issues, we need to understand certain functions of religious temples in the city, the focal point of Paul's discussion. Several temples in Corinth had dining rooms where religious feasts were often held. These feasts were important social occasions in the city. These temples functioned almost like restaurants for the prominent citizens.[4] The meals served in these temples, however, had a religious character about them. Plutarch said, "It is not the abundance of wine or the roasting of meat that makes the joy of festivals, but the good hope and belief that the god is present in his kindness and graciously accepts what is offered."[5] In spite of the clear religious overtones of the meals in these temples, some of the Christians insisted on eating there. This was part of their life and their culture. They had no intention of giving it up.

These individuals prided themselves in their knowledge and, in their knowledge, freedom. They knew that idols were not gods. They saw nothing wrong with eating meals in the temples. Paul, on the other hand, strictly forbids them from eating in the temples (10:14-22). There are demons present in the religious feasts, Paul argues. He forbids them to participate in such an activity. But there is a difference between eating food in the temples themselves and eating the temple meat at home (10:25-30).

Paul is greatly concerned about some in the church he calls "weak" (8:7-13). We typically call morally weak those who have few scruples. Paul, in this context, uses the term to describe those with a superabundance of scruples. These were more than likely lower-class

Christians and slaves who were unable to afford meat on a regular basis. Eating meat for them was rare. Eating at a temple dining room was not a real option for them. For that reason, while wealthier Christians would have likely eaten temple meals commonly, poorer Christians would have known little about them except what they would have experienced at some temple feast or holy day in the temple prior to their conversion. Eating any sort of meat associated with the temple, even if it were bought at the public marketplace, would always carry for them a special religious association.[6]

Paul sides with neither group. His position depended upon whether the "idol meat" was purchased at the market or eaten at a temple feast. On one hand, Paul says that meat bought in the market was only meat. It was unnecessary to scrutinize where it came from (10:25, 26). On the other hand, Paul forbids them from participating in the temple meals (8:10; 10:20-22). But the primary issue at hand is not about eating meat. His argument goes directly toward those who ate the temple meals, the well-to-do members who apparently were causing the problems in their assemblies as well. These people, who prided themselves in their knowledge, saw freedom as the greatest of virtues. Their concern over their social standing and personal fulfillment drove them toward behavior they thought was best for themselves without concern for its impact on others. Paul says that love, not freedom, is the basis for Christian living and that, rather than focusing on individual fulfillment, the guiding force for Christian living should be what is best for the community.

This is not a minor point. The behavior of those who insisted on their freedom was jeopardizing the very faith of those whom they were influencing. The issue is clear in 8:10: "If others see you, who possess knowledge, eating in the temple of an idol, might they not, since their conscience is weak, be encouraged to the point of eating food sacrificed to idols?" In other words, wouldn't they be encouraged to transgress against what they believe is sinful? "So by your knowledge," he says, "those weak believers for whom Christ died are destroyed." When these so-called knowledgeable Christians hurt those with a weak conscience in this way, they are not just sinning against their fellow Christians; they are sinning against Christ

(8:11, 12). Would they be willing to relinquish their freedom for the sake of others in the community, for the sake of Christ himself?

To modern Christians, the issue of eating meat in a temple seems odd. Perhaps an analogy would help. If a newspaper and magazine shop were housed in a store known widely for selling pornography, would Christians understand if they were told they shouldn't go there, even if they were only buying *Newsweek* or *Better Homes and Gardens*? Would they understand how in exercising their freedom they might unintentionally lead weaker brothers and sisters to sin? Could they distinguish between what was sold and where it was sold? While this is not an exact parallel, it might help in understanding why Paul saw temple meals as an important issue for Christians.

These table issues, however, were only part of what divided the church. It was fragmented in several ways. Paul's purpose in this letter is stated clearly: "I appeal to you, brothers and sisters, by the name of our Lord Jesus Christ, that all of you be in agreement and that there be no divisions among you, but that you be united in the same mind and the same purpose" (1 Cor. 1:10). People from Chloe's household reported quarrels among them (1:11). One group claims allegiance to Paul, another to Apollos, another to Cephas, another, smugly perhaps, to Christ. These groups, which more than likely represented house churches around the city, have divided the very body of Christ. The quarrelling, Paul says, grows out of human inclinations, not godly ones (3:3).

Moreover, an argument has broken out between the tongue-speakers and the prophets, and this issue has added to the disorder taking place in the assembly (1 Cor. 12-14). Each group claimed superiority over the other. Those who spoke, or more accurately prayed (14:2), in tongues exercised an individual gift. They were the only ones edified in the exercise of this gift. It was neither intelligible nor edifying to the church. Its use, apart from interpretation, was a sign of judgment to the unbelievers (14:22) since the outsiders could not understand it and were thus excluded.

In contrast, Paul urges everyone to seek the gift of prophecy (14:1). This gift was a word of instruction (14:19) that functioned to build up, encourage, or console the church (14:3). It was a communal gift, that is, for the benefit of the whole church. Of course, it did not come with inherent personal authority. It had to be weighed and discerned (14:29), and if it were unintelligible or did not build up the church, it suffered from the same problem as tongue speaking. For this and many other reasons the Christian assembly at Corinth had become a place of disorder and divisive behavior.

Paul is aghast at the behavior he sees tearing the church apart at Corinth. Not only were the Christians quarreling, some were engaged in substantial breaches of moral standards. One man is having sexual relations with his stepmother while the church sits on the sidelines without comment. Some are tarnishing the name of Christ through lawsuits against other Christians. Others are having sexual relations with prostitutes. Paul believed these divisions and the acceptance of destructive and immoral behavior threatened the future of the church. The church cannot continue living this way. He turns to address the root problem.

THE ROAD UNTRAVELED

The Corinthian Christians have been pursuing two paths. One Paul calls the way of signs, that is, the way of power, of experience, of the public demonstration of the working of the Holy Spirit. This way has led them to their attraction to the more public gifts and has pitted the more prominent gifts against each other to the detriment of the whole church. The other Paul calls the way of wisdom, that is, the way of special knowledge, of intellectual attainment and superiority. This way has isolated the haves from the have-nots, the knows from the know-nothings.

Paul condemns both of these ways. Both are self-oriented. Both are divisive. Neither partakes of the spirit of Christ. He calls them not to a middle way, not to a sort of balanced mixture of signs and wisdom. He calls them, rather, to a third way, a way they have never seriously pursued, a way with a radically different starting point and that creates a radically different community—the way of the cross (1:18, 23; 2:2). This is what he preached when he was with them; this was the basis of their salvation. And though it is a stumbling block to those who seek signs and scandalous to those who seek wisdom, it is God's power and his wisdom. It is God's only way.

This is no theoretical argument. Had they grasped the way of the cross, it would have changed how they did church. Actually the reverse is truer, and here is the point: if they changed how they did church, they could grasp the way of the cross, or be grasped by it. If their assemblies reflected a different center and if their worship pointed to a different kind of relationship, they could become people of the cross as God intended. But they would have to rethink how they ate and drank together. They must no longer come together piecemeal but as community. Hear Paul's argument beginning in 11:17.

In the following instructions I am not going to praise you. When all of you come together, your assemblies are not making things better but are making them worse. You come together as a whole church, which is ironic since your actions indicate you don't care about the whole church. You come together as factions, which means that for at least some of you, your discipleship is not genuine. Sure, you assemble together but for all the wrong reasons. You don't seem to care about the "together" part, only being with people like yourselves. You come to participate in the Supper, but let's be clear: it is not the Lord's Supper you eat but a Self Supper. When the time comes to eat, you all eat your own supper.

You seem to think this is about you, about what you want and like. Some gorge themselves while others go away hungry, and you don't even seem to notice. You come to share in the cup, but some of you drink so much you get drunk. Is this all the supper means to you? Do you think this is one of your dinner parties? If this is just about eating and drinking, you have homes to do that in, don't you? Some of you eat and drink and enjoy yourself and are oblivious that you are showing contempt for God's church by humiliating those who have nothing. Do you see them? Do you even care? Do you want me to congratulate you about how well the Lord's Supper is going, how well you are doing church? I do not congratulate you at all!

When I was with you I shared with you what I had received from the Lord. Had you grasped this and lived by it, you wouldn't be in the mess you are in; so listen. On the night he was betrayed, the Lord Jesus took a loaf of bread. He gave thanks for it and broke it. He said to his disciples, "This is my body that is for you. Do this in *anamnesis* of me."

Paul's readers would have understood this point. No definitions would have been needed. Modern readers in English, however, are at a disadvantage because of how our language has evolved. *Anamnesis*, or remembrance, is not about recalling an event that took place a long time ago. It is about fully experiencing it again. The Passover meal, which served as the immediate context of Jesus' last supper with his disciples, was marked by *anamnesis*. Participants in the meal, both then and now, do not merely recall God's past deliverance but claim that very deliverance for themselves. It did not happen only to their ancient ancestors but also to them. The language is first person. "God saw us in slavery. He delivered us, gave us his law, protected us, and provided for us the land of promise." To remember is to experience again the full power and significance of a past event.

Similarly, to participate in *anamnesis* is not simply to talk about an event but to reenact it in substantial ways. If I were to ask my mother, for example, what her wedding was like, she could, of course, tell me stories about it. This is certainly what I would expect. But, I suppose, she could also do it another way. She could say, "Wait right here." In a few minutes she returns and Dad is with her. Mom is wearing the wedding dress she wore in 1941. Dad is in a suit. Several of her old attendants come into the room wearing their bridesmaids' dresses. She positions them where they would have been on that day sixty-four years ago. She and Dad make their vows to each other again. That's more than an explanation. They have reenacted the event, re-embodied it. I would understand her wedding differently. So it is with the Supper. The death of Jesus is reenacted and re-experienced.

The words "Do This in Remembrance of Me" are carved into the wood of the communion tables in many churches. These words do not say "Think This" but rather "Do This" even though most of us do a lot of thinking and very little doing when we participate in the Lord's Supper. Do what? Do *anamnesis*. Participate in remembrance. In the taking of the bread and the drinking of the cup, we re-experience the death and resurrection event. We don't just think quietly to ourselves about what happened to Jesus a long time ago. We don't just tell a story or two about it. We rehearse it, we reenact it, we re-embody it. And the very power that nailed our sins to the cross, the power that rolled the stone away from the empty tomb, breathes into our lungs and transforms us into the people of God.

Paul is doing more than just reminding the Corinthians of what happened three decades before. He is taking this group of broken Christians and recasting them into the shape of the cross. So he continues.

> Jesus blessed the bread and said, "This is my body that is for you. Do this in *anamnesis* of me." In the same way after supper Jesus took the cup and said, "This cup is the new covenant of my blood. Every time you drink it, do so in remembrance of me." Dear Corinthians, if you miss this point, you miss everything. Whenever you come together to sit at table with each other, whenever you eat of this bread and drink of this cup, you are proclaiming, you are exhibiting, the Lord's death until he comes.
>
> In the supper you are re-experiencing the crucifixion of Christ. Christ gave himself up for you. Christ relinquished his freedoms, including the freedom to live, and he did so for your sake. The way he died challenges you to give yourself up, to relinquish your freedoms for the sake of others. Everything about the cross cuts against the grain of your self-serving behavior. Stop thinking about yourself and start caring about everyone else who comes to the table with you.
>
> So I'm asking you to examine yourselves. Scrutinize what you are doing. Whoever eats the bread or drinks the cup

in an unworthy manner will be answerable for the body and blood of the Lord. What manner of eating and drinking is unworthy? Let me be clear. I am not talking about whether you come to the table as sinners. Of course you are sinners. None of you is worthy of what Christ has done. I am talking about something else entirely. If your participation in the bread and cup is self-serving, if you are oblivious to everyone else present, if you go on with your own meal and leave others out, if you are not observant of, or do not care about, the body of Christ present with you, then you eat and drink judgment on yourselves.

In the Supper you encounter Christ's body—Christ's body broken on the cross for you and Christ's broken body sitting at table with you. The church is the body of Christ. When you ignore the others at table with you, you ignore Christ. When you reject them by serving them leftovers or sending them home hungry, you dishonor the cross itself. No wonder so many of you are weak and ill. Your behavior has been toxic for the whole church, and it is affecting everything. So I say to you, when you all come together to eat, wait for each other, serve each other, be aware of each other, care for each other. By this you will embody the cross of Christ until he returns.

Their meal had become symptomatic of their problems, but it was also their hope. Here was an opportunity to serve. Here the rich could welcome the poor, masters could honor slaves, men could affirm women, and the strong could minister to the weak. If all were received at table, if all were fed and all were respected, the very character of the church would change. Those who possessed knowledge would no longer exalt their freedom but would relinquish their rights if others were being caused to sin. The gifted would no longer use their gifts for their own honor. The church would no longer clamor after signs or pride themselves in wisdom, but they would seek a third way, a radically different way. In the Supper, by God's power, they would become people of the cross.

IN THE ABSENCE OF SUFFERING

I have often wondered what went wrong in the church in Corinth that made its problems so substantial. Almost every church we know of in the first century experienced tension and conflict, but none of them approach the level of fragmentation we see among the Corinthians. What were the unique circumstances of this church that promoted its quarrels and divisions?

The answer is revealing for modern churches. Unlike the other churches we know about in the first century, the church in Corinth experienced comparatively little conflict with outsiders.[7] The ramifications of that insight are significant. While correspondence with virtually every other church reveals that early Christians lived at odds with prevailing cultural values, there is little hint in the Corinthian letters that they were suffering in any way at the hands of outsiders. Wealthier members of the church continued their civic and social life without great impact on their lifestyle. The poor suffered about as much in the church as they did in the city. Even church meals resembled Corinthian dinner parties. The tensions normally felt by Christians in relation to the culture were largely missing here.

In the absence of those tensions, the Corinthians quarreled among themselves. They did not pursue lifestyles that contrasted to the prevailing values. They had little fear of being ostracized, much less persecuted, by the citizens of Corinth. As they lived largely by Corinthian standards and imbibed deeply the cultural mores around them, or better said, because they did, they quarreled among themselves and often treated each other shamefully.

Paul's rhetoric, then, was not simply to correct them but to create in them a different reality. It was to shape their values not as the people of Corinth but as citizens of a different city. He spoke of a wisdom "not of this age or of the rulers of this age, who are doomed to perish" (2:6). God's wisdom would not be discernible in Corinthian academies or widely accepted in the streets. Rather God's wisdom is "secret and hidden" (2:7). We Christians "have received not the spirit of the world, but that Spirit that is from God.... And we speak of these things in words not taught by human wisdom but taught by the Spirit" (2:13). They needed to see the world differently, and they needed to see themselves in relation to the world differently. If they did, they would not be the same. If they ever saw what they were fighting against, they would work to find themselves in agreement concerning the things that mattered, they would discover the common mind that they shared in Christ, and they would stop quarreling.

I am not sure, but I think this may be part of the problem modern Christians face, especially in America. We lived for a long time under the illusion that our nation was generally Christian, that the values of the surrounding culture paralleled, if not complemented, our own. Christians in business or education, journalism or medicine, could live lives virtually indistinguishable from those who were not Christians. We cared generally about the same things, worried about the same issues, pursued the same wealth, and reflected the same values about race and politics. Few Christians felt estranged from their neighbors. Few had to defend their lifestyle or their choices. We bought in to the American Dream and reaped its ostensible benefits. We lived at peace with the world.

As a consequence perhaps, we quarreled with each other. While we did good works, built great edifices, expanded missions, and gave to the poor, we also held people at arm's distance, became suspicious, labeled, blamed, and accused. When it came to differences among us, a spirit of debate not dialogue became the norm. Like the Christians in Corinth, we divided over issues that were petty and small while we lived in relative peace with the world.

AT THE TABLE OF PEACE

To the church's great benefit the relationship of Christians to the prevailing culture is changing. Being a Christian is no longer socially advantageous. Many believers are viewed with suspicion and even contempt, or, worse, they are marginalized or ignored. Fifty years ago, evangelism in America was often treated as a matter of changing the doctrinal perspectives of those who believed they were already Christians. While that approach might have had its problems then, in our current situation it is often counterproductive or even absurd. I am not saying that discussions about doctrine are no longer necessary. They are. But it is clearer now that many of our friends and neighbors don't need merely to adjust their beliefs a little; they need to be converted to Jesus. I believe this may be true for many in the church as well. In such a context, some of the things we have argued about fade into insignificance, or at least they should.

Here in this crucial moment is an opportunity for the church to come together in family reunion, telling the kinds of stories only close families can tell. Here is an opening for the gospel of peace. Christians who are overwhelmed by the world's seductions, wealthy Christians who are weary of trying to keep up, poor Christians who feel keenly the burdens of daily living, all come together for worship and encouragement. Those who are older put aside their fears and preferences. Those who are younger share their temptations and their dreams. Here in the assembly, they all receive the word of God by which they may be convicted and changed. They all offer their prayers because their needs are great. Then the whole church joins together—young and old, the working class and professionals, blacks and whites, women and men, people who bring with them profound differences of perspective and understanding—to welcome one another, to embrace rather than reject, to kiss rather than quarrel. Everything that divides, that marks some as less worthy or desirable, is set aside. They extend to each other the peace of Christ.

Then all come to the table. Here the body broken and fragmented, sinful and needy, encounters the broken body of Christ, perfect and holy, slain and resurrected. Here the church sings out its assent with the amen. Here strangers come together as family. Here the stories are told and the family connections are made. Here the death of Christ is remembered, the power of the cross fully experienced. Here we learn at last who we are. At the table enemies are reconciled and a covenant is confirmed. At the table walls are torn down and arguments rested, hearts mended and wounds salved. At the table the whole church comes to offer its sins and receive forgiveness, to eat the bread of hope and drink the medicine of immortality. At the table, the gathered church breaks the bread so that its own brokenness might be healed. At the table Christians, bloodied by conflict within and hostilities without, drink the blood of Christ and receive his protection and care.

Relentlessly pursued by spiritual forces of darkness, we race to the head tent and pull aside its curtains. There the host embraces us and invites us to sit with his family. We join the meal. Our enemies are rebuffed. We have not come to this sanctuary alone. We have joined all nations and all races. We come as poor, blind, imperfect, and needy, as unholy, unworthy, and unclean. But we are received as daughters and sons of the king. The shroud that has covered us is removed. Death is devoured and life is given, enmity is crushed and peace is granted, because here, at the table, we are welcomed by the exalted Son to eat and drink with our God.

NOTES

1. William Willimon, *Sunday Dinner* (Nashville: The Upper Room, 1981), 16.

2. This composite picture comes from a variety of sources. The best and earliest picture of what happens in Christian assemblies, outside the small amount of information we have in the New Testament, comes from Justin Martyr in the middle of the second century, about a generation after the last apostle had died. See especially *1 Apology* 66, 67, *Dialogue* 41, 70. See also the prayer of eucharist in the *Didache* 9 from the late first century and Pliny's *Letter to Trajan* (*Letters*, 10.97) ca. 112. Among numerous helpful secondary sources are *Liturgies of the Western Church*, introduced and compiled by Bard Thompson (Philadelphia: Fortress, 1961); Larry Hurtado, *At the Origins of Christian Worship* (Grand Rapids: Eerdmans, 1999); and Allen Cabaniss, *Pattern in Early Christian Worship* (Macon, GA: Mercer University Press, 1989).

3. For helpful discussions of these issues, see Ben Witherington III, *Conflict and Community in Corinth* (Grand Rapids: Eerdmans), 1996, and Robert Banks, *Paul's Idea of Community: The Early House Churches in Their Historical Setting* (Grand Rapids: Eerdmans, 1980).

4. Ben Witherington III, *Conflict and Community in Corinth*, 188.

5. *Moralia*, 1102A.

6. Gerd Theissen, *The Social Setting of Pauline Christianity: Essays on Corinth* (Philadelphia: Westminster, 1982), 121ff.

7. See especially James Walters, "Civic Identity in Roman Corinth and Its Impact on Early Christians," in *Urban Religion in Roman Corinth: Interdisciplinary Approaches*, Daniel Schowalter and Steven J. Friesen, eds. (Cambridge: Harvard University Press, 2005), 1-21.

CHAPTER SEVEN

A COMMUNITY OF BROKENNESS

The Inbreaking of the Peace of Christ

Fear dictates two modes of behavior: violence and rigidity.

—Jacques Ellul

The highest of all is not to understand the highest
but to act upon it.

—Soren Kierkegaard

Fear filled my chest and squeezed my heart so tight that I thought for sure it would stop beating. I sat in bed, squinting through the door into the next room lit dimly by moonlight. I tried to make out any unusual shapes or unwelcome movement. I am absolutely certain I had heard footsteps.

I was working on my writing project, staying by myself in a small ranch house south of Abilene. The charming three-room dwelling is nestled in hills adorned with the subtle colors and sweet scent of mesquite and cedar. Anyone walking through one of the green valleys or viewing the hills surrounding the ranch would be captivated.

The house was ideal for my purposes. My work required time alone, time to think, time to pray, time to be creative without interruption by cell phone or television. But I am a city boy used to night sounds that do not resemble the noises made by the insects and wild animals that inhabit the area. I normally fall asleep to the comforting sounds of trains hitching and unhitching their cars, automobile stereos with bass boosters on hyper-drive playing the latest thrash metal tunes, and the soothing sounds of my wife's rhythmic breathing. She, on the other hand, prepares to sleep accompanied by different breathing noises, some of which remind her of gasoline-powered chain saws, gurgling fountains, and the sonorous tones of large flatulent mammals, against which she braces herself with a full arsenal of sensory deprivation gear.

I thought I was mentally prepared to go to bed alone that first night out in the country. I had worked on the manuscript until after midnight. I was barely conscious when I pulled back the covers. I plugged speakers into my laptop, opened my iTunes, cranked the sound up on my favorite Dave Matthews album, and fell asleep during one of Dave's falsetto trips in "Warehouse." When I awakened a couple of hours later, I was in a cold sweat. I listened to the footsteps shuffling through the next room. Who could it be? What were they looking for? How could they have found this place so isolated from civilization? Did they know I was here? My mind raced. It would be days before anyone found my body.

Finally, with an act of uncharacteristic courage, I jumped out of bed, brandishing one of the white Avia tennis shoes that had been resting nearby. I turned on the light and faced the empty room. After checking the water heater closet, bathroom, shower, pantry, front porch, and, finally, under the bed, I sheepishly snuggled the shoe next to its mate and slipped back under the covers, leaving most of the lights on. I listened to the wind blow the mesquite branches against the house until just after dawn.

FEAR AND FRAGMENTATION

Fear is paralyzing and debilitating. It turns rational thought into Play Dough. Under the power of fear, human beings who are otherwise normal do odd things. They suspend good judgment, jump to false conclusions, and anticipate unimaginable consequences. The overriding impulse is self-protection, sometimes at any cost, even if the behavior seems foolish or peculiar to others.

Take, for example, our friend Samuel. A few months ago he took Jeanene and me to the great Canopy Walkway high atop the trees in Kakum National Park in Ghana. Samuel is a man of great strength, physically and spiritually. He has an imposing presence, a commanding voice, and a confident manner that can manage almost any situation. He is principal of a college in Ghana, a powerful preacher, and a dear friend. But when it comes to heights, his spine is the consistency of homemade yogurt. The rope bridges at Kakum hang about two hundred feet above the jungle floor, suspended from tree to tree. We watched as school children scurried across, waving cheerily to their parents. We saw a white-haired woman stop every few feet, hanging over the edge taking pictures in every direction. Samuel smiled and told us he would meet us at the end of the walkway. The last time he had come, he had actually gotten a few feet out on the latticework before crawling on his belly back to firm ground while pre-school children prepared to step over his body and onto the rope bridge. After we completed our treetop tour, we were welcomed at the end by Samuel's broad grin.

All of us understand such fear and can tell our own stories. Fear is a potent emotion that both empowers and inhibits decisive action. Rightly viewed, fear is a gift from God. When it fills its proper role, it serves as fuel for the body during a crisis. It provides strength we didn't know we had. It sharpens our minds and eliminates distractions. It performs triage on our priorities. Under the influence of fear, we realize some things just don't seem very important while others command our attention and energies.

But sometimes fear debilitates and makes constructive responses difficult. Unconstrained fear causes us to lose perspective. It obscures our judgment by marginalizing insights that might have been helpful had we taken the time to consider them. When we live with fear for long periods of time, our vision is affected. We lose sight of things. We grow tired. We lose patience.

Fear can be especially dysfunctional at its extremes. At one end, fear drives us to hurt others. We lash out against people we think threaten us, people we don't understand or who are not like us. We criticize or disparage others out of our instincts to protect ourselves or those we love. At the other end, fear paralyzes us. We shut others out. We become isolated, seeking the familiar to provide us a measure of comfort and to shield us from what frightens us. At both extremes, constructive engagement with others is impeded. Left to overflow its banks, running wild through fields and villages, fear causes great destruction. The debris from the flood of our fear is not difficult to see. It is evident in hurt eyes, excessive caution, damaged reputations, indecision, and sometimes reprisal. When it affects the church, the consequences can be devastating.

I suspect much of the fragmentation the church is experiencing is the result of fear. I don't know for sure. Certainly some people are afraid. They are afraid of change, or they are afraid that change won't happen fast enough. Some are losing power and influence. Others fear that the church as they have always known it is going away. Whatever its cause, unchecked and unexamined, fear can destroy churches. In many places it already has. Unconstrained fear makes us judgmental and impatient. Its instincts are to talk about rather than to talk with. It undermines friendships and victimizes the innocent. It pushes some down and pushes others away. While perfect love casts out fear, fear unrestrained by love casts out people.

Through years of ministry, I have not known how to address fear when I have encountered it, partly because I was so afraid myself. I was afraid of doing the wrong thing or making the wrong decision. I was afraid of criticism and afraid of confrontation. I would by lying if I somehow indicated that I am no longer afraid. But over time my perspective has changed. Like a nurse who is no longer squeamish at the sight of blood, I am no longer so afraid. It is not that I have grown calloused. I pray that this is not so. Rather, I have learned to see people differently. After holding the hand of a young man with colon cancer as he took his last breath, after preaching the funerals of three-year-olds and young mothers, after walking through the divorces of friends and family, after seeing the human wreckage of sexual abuse and the devastation of racism, after receiving too many anonymous letters challenging my sanity or my faith, after hearing verbal attacks in the back foyer and curt words over the phone, after witnessing lives being destroyed through the abusive behavior of church members in the name of discipline and accountability, I have had my eyes opened to the frailty of the human condition and the sheer brokenness of Christ's church.

To see with such eyes is liberating because it allows me to see others as I wish to be seen—as a hurting, broken, and sinful man in need of affirmation and care. At my best self, I no longer see dangerous enemies who oppose me but hurting people who deserve my kindness and my prayers. I see people who are powerless or afraid, people who are protecting their loved ones and their future as well as safeguarding their understanding of the gospel. In other words, the more I look, the more I see people like me. I am a member of a community of brokenness. With that awareness comes the task of granting to others what I have received: grace and peace.

All our churches are fractured communities. They are not gated neighborhoods or walled fortresses. They are not businesses or civic organizations. Rather, they are hospitals for the weak and the lost; they are infirmaries for the sinful and the hopeless. What complicates matters, of course, is that we are all patients. Some may walk around with white coats and clipboards. Some will claim to be wise. Others will try to exercise power. A few may even try to dismiss some of the other patients. But none of us should be fooled. There is only one physician, only one expert in what makes people ill, only one with any real authority. The rest of us are in need of care. Some may be in the cancer ward and others in the coronary care unit, but whatever our appearance, we are all sick. There are certainly things we should fear, but the other patients should not be among them.

Recognizing ourselves in fractured communities provides a change of perspective. Our fear is a symptom of our brokenness. Our brokenness is an opportunity for grace. And grace is the spring from which peacemaking always flows.

New Eyes, New Heart

I have been determined not to offer simple steps for becoming peacemakers. I have avoided trying to give ready answers for the things that ail us. I don't know all those answers, and following sure-fire steps in something this complex usually misfires. The ministry of reconciliation is messy business. Ultimately, only God can fix us. But certain attitudes and commitments will open our hearts to embrace the peace of Christ. I will mention three.

The person who can most bring peace to a church is the one who has a heart for confession. Confession serves as an antidote to fear. It prepares the soil of our hearts to cultivate love, which, in turn, nudges fear aside. It puts us in our proper place. It defines who we are. Perhaps, it defines who we are not. We confess that we are not God. We confess that God is sovereign and that Jesus is Lord, which is to say, we confess our inadequacies, our foolishness, and our dependence. We are not in charge. On our own we are unholy people in need of redemption, unworthy people in need of care. We are sinners all.

Confession is not merely for the guy with serious sins, the one who comes forward after the sermon to fill out a card and receive prayers, the one we sometimes whisper about wondering exactly what he did to merit being paraded in front of the whole church, the one that reminds us that we never want to do anything so bad. Rather confession is for all of us. We all have serious sins. We all need to confess publicly that Jesus is Lord and that we are not. We all engage in thoughts and actions that are unworthy of the God who has saved us.

We come together not to sing our favorite songs or to tell God what we want but in order to surrender. Church is the place that Christians assemble so that we might lay down our arms. We convene with white flags in our hands. We have nothing with which to negotiate, nothing to offer God that merits his attention, much less his generosity. Gathered in worship, an unholy people stand naked and needy in the face of a holy God. In that encounter something remarkable happens. Weak, sinful, divided, frustrated, petty people are renewed as the holy, chosen, sinless, united, gracious people of God.

As we come together and as we look at each other, our eyes are not hard. There is a softness around the edges, kindness in the wrinkles. It hasn't always been that way for us, of course. As Paul told the

Corinthians, we used to see one another with human eyes, but we do so no longer. Christ has given us new eyes. Now we see fellow sufferers who are frail and sick. We see patients with gangrened limbs and serious conditions of the heart. We look behind the anger and the gossip and see people made sick by legalism or paralyzed by fear. We look behind the smugness and the cynicism and see people with too many wounds and too few friends who have noticed or cared. We see the powerless and the helpless, the injured and the lost. They have burdens to carry, for those who have eyes to see. Here, I believe, is where peace begins.

COMING TO OUR SENSES

If we are to live as people of peace, a second commitment is needed. Before we can become the people God made us, we need to repent. I hesitate to use this word because it is off-putting to modern Christians. It is a hard word, but for many reasons it is the right word. It is what we and our churches need desperately.

Repentance is not merely a preparatory step before baptism, quickly taken then promptly forgotten once we towel off. Nor is it a behavior relegated to rogues and scoundrels whose sawdust-trail conversions are the lore of tent revivals and gospel campaigns. Rather repentance is how Christians live normally. It is the base line for our discipleship. It provides urgency to our actions and energy for our prayers. Repentance calls God's people to walk alongside the Prodigal, gazing anxiously toward home. We see what we had not seen before: we have not just broken our Father's rules; we have broken his heart.

I like how Frederick Buechner has put it: "To repent is to come to your senses. It is not so much something you do as something that happens. True repentance spends less time looking at the past and saying, 'I'm sorry,' than to the future and saying, 'Wow!'"[1] These words stop me in my tracks every time I read them. That's partly, I suppose, because I am very quick to say I'm sorry. I don't mean that I shouldn't be sorry or that I shouldn't express it. But sometimes saying I'm sorry is just too easy. It's a sort of cut-rate repentance. And sometimes it is not repentance at all.

If my wife tells me about a tough situation she has experienced, perhaps a difficult conversation with a student, my first instinct is to respond, "I'm sorry." In those moments she often looks at me with an expression that says, "Were you even listening to what I was telling you? You weren't in this story. How could you be sorry for any of it?" It is not that I was feeling guilty about anything. It's just that I want everything to be all right for her. I don't want her to feel bad. Telling her how sorry I am allows me to cover all my bases. "I'm sorry" in those moments means "Take these little words and make them mean whatever it is that would make you feel better now." This is not repentance; it's pacification.

Even when I am truly guilty, even when apologizing is crucial for making things right, a quick "I'm sorry" is not enough. At least two deeper things are needed. One is genuine remorse, a heart that is broken at the wound I have inflicted. This response is more than just feeling bad about things. It is recognizing my culpability in the situation. The guilt of my own actions washes over me so that I am no longer focused on what the other has done to me, but I am over-whelmed at what I have done or who I have become. Repentance is serious medicine with serious effects. Repentance requires me to suffer embarrassment and perhaps even shame. I am convinced that one of the reasons peacemaking is so rare is that repentance is so painful. What is surprising, perhaps, is how unwilling many Christians are to endure pain for the sake of the larger good, which is to say for the sake of following Christ. Pain is part of the cost of being a disciple but one that many of us have not counted. If repentance is necessary for being a peacemaker, no wonder few of us are blessed.

Beyond saying "I'm sorry," we need a second deep response. Repentance calls me to re-envision the relationship, to imagine what the "new us" looks like and then live it. To see a new reality birthed out of the dead skin of the old is to have one's eyes opened. It is to see not just the possibilities but the reality of something new, something good, not in the distant future but in the here and now, even as things are being worked out, even as the conflict unfolds. Repentance invites us to envision a new relationship, a new community, and a new way of acting. Just as the Prodigal knew everything was different when he saw his father running toward him, so we, when we come to our senses, are able to look past the pain and see the work of God in our midst. Something extraordinary is taking place, perhaps even miraculous. Then the exclamation of repentance is not so much "I'm sorry" but "Wow!"

LIVING AS IF

The recognition that God is working out of our confession and surrender and through our repentance opens up a third commitment by which we become a people of peace: we are called to live "as if." We acknowledge that the church that is in God's heart does not exist here, not as we are living it. Christians still sin. The church is still divided. Christians do not talk well across racial and cultural borders. Congregations are often marked by unhealthy talk and destructive behavior. We all play our part. We all suffer.

As recipients of the righteousness of God, which he has given us as a free gift, we are empowered to live as if. We live as if the church were a community of care and compassion. We live as if the walls were torn down. We live as if there were no cultural barriers. We may not know how our neighbors will respond to our attempts at hospitality or our acts of service, but that is not our concern. We live as if they will respond with graciousness and thanksgiving, and if they do not we serve them anyway. In the same way that God treats us as if we were deserving of his mercy, we treat others with kindness and understanding no matter how they act. Our speech is soft. Our words are kind. Our tone is gentle. Our prayers are persistent.

Over time, by God's grace, "living as if" becomes "living as reality." Our behaviors become habit; our new actions become our spiritual instincts. We create for ourselves and for our neighbors the possibility of a new world, a new identity. I am not arguing for a sanctified version of "act your way into a better way of feeling" or "fake it until you make it." Rather I am urging us toward authentic behavior that reflects the self-emptying character of Christ. When we serve others who do not serve us, we embody Christ. When we treat with kindness those who are unkind, we incarnate Christ. When we forgive others who have not sought or deserved our forgiveness, we reflect the very nature of Christ. Over time by such actions, hearts are changed, including our own.

"Living as if" does not mean that we live naively or without discernment. We live with wisdom and with kingdom shrewdness, which is not to say with cynicism or manipulation. We do not pretend people are not being hurt. We do not lose our ability to see and respond to racism, sexism, hatred, or abuse. We are not blind to those who would destroy the body of Christ such as the deceivers in John's community who did not confess that Jesus came in the flesh (2 John 7-11) or the blatantly immoral man in Corinth who was living with his father's wife (1 Cor. 5:1-5) or the lawkeepers in the Galatian churches who were undermining the gospel of grace and were, thereby, preaching a different gospel (Gal. 1:6-9). Our eyes are wide open. We can still see what's going on. We are braced against sin. Some people's behaviors are so destructive or their doctrines so alien to the gospel that they should be dealt with firmly and decisively, for their sakes as well as the church's. Even then, however, our responses are gracious and our speech seasoned with salt. All of our instincts are aroused with compassion in the face of the sin of others just as Christ was aroused with compassion in the face of our own. Though others may treat us unfairly, we choose to respond in mercy. Though others may gossip, we choose to speak with sensitivity or not to speak at all. When we are sinned against, we do not respond in kind but with gentleness and grace.

How often must we forgive the one who has injured us, Peter asked. As many as seven times? Not just seven, Jesus answered, but seventy times seven (Matt. 18:22). Forgiveness has no upper limit and no statute of limitation. We forgive others as God has forgiven us, innumerably and infinitely. No matter what others have done, we see them as if their slate were clean, as if they had treated us with kindness and mercy. If we don't, not only is the work of the church hindered, we ourselves are left wounded and bruised.

A community of brokenness is filled with fractured people whom Christ has given eyes to see. We no longer view others as destructive people who hurt us but as weak people who need us. We live as if they were forgiven, and over time they become truly forgiven in our hearts. Over time, perhaps, they become for us what they have been all along in Christ's eyes: godly men and women, our brothers and sisters, sinners forgiven by God.

IRENIC ABSENCE

Participating in the ministry of peacemaking within our communities of brokenness is about both what we do and what we choose not to do. Most often we think of peacemaking as engaging in constructive actions in relation to others. We confess our weaknesses and sins. We live in communities of faith with hearts of repentance. We treat others every day as if they were loving and kind. But while the ministry of godly presence is the primary soil in which peacemaking occurs, there are times that peace is served only through disengaging from others, through an irenic absence.

I was a grown man before I first heard the word "irenic." I was a graduate student when a guest lecturer used the word in one of my classes. I don't remember much about his remarks. I just remember thinking at the time that the poor fellow didn't know how to pronounce "ironic." Maybe he's British, I thought. Upon hearing it a second time a few weeks later, I decided to look it up. Since then it has become one of my most cherished words.

Irenic comes from the Greek word *eirene*, which means peace. People who are irenic promote peace. They are bridge builders, they love their enemies, they are slow to be angry and quick to encourage. Sometimes, however, a situation is so intractable or people's behavior is so destructive that disengagement from the dialogue is necessary so that peace might prevail.

Such is the case in Paul's exhortation to Timothy. Throughout his correspondence with his young protégé, Paul urges Timothy to lead the church in promoting healthy teaching, what in some English versions is translated "sound doctrine." Some things build up the church; others tear it down. Healthy teaching edifies and encourages the church. Some at Ephesus, apparently including some of the elders as well as some of the women, were undoing with their tongues the peace of Christ. This is in part why Paul says that an elder must manage his own household well (1 Tim. 3:4, 5). If he cannot respond well to destructive behavior in his own family, how can he do so in the church?

Among the elements of their unhealthy teaching were a morbid craving for controversy, disputes about words, dissension, slander, base suspicions, and wrangling among Christians, some of whom were looking for financial advantage (1 Tim. 6:4, 5). Two men were engaged in unhealthy teaching by saying that the resurrection had already occurred (2 Tim. 2:17, 18). Whatever approaches Timothy might use to deal with such issues, Paul tells him to avoid disputing about words because they don't do any good but only ruin the hearers (2 Tim. 2:14). He urges him to handle the word of truth rightly, that is, to communicate constructively, irenically (2 Tim. 2:15). To do that, he must avoid godless chatter because it leads people into more ungodliness, because it works in a church like gangrene in a sick body (2 Tim. 2:16, 17). Paul tells Timothy to have nothing to do with stupid, senseless controversies because these breed quarrels, and God's children are not quarrelsome. Rather, the servant of God is kind to everyone, teaches well, is forbearing, and corrects opponents with gentleness (2 Tim. 2:23, 24).

For Paul communication is about building up, not tearing down. Healthy speech—in other words, sound doctrine—strengthens rather than destroys. And if healthy speech is not possible, if continuation in the dialogue means further controversy or more quarreling, then irenic Christians should back away. As hard as it is not to speak, for the sake of the health of the church, Christians sometimes have to keep their mouths shut. They must engage in an irenic absence from unhealthy conversations so that the church is not damaged by destructive talk.

Irenic absence should not be confused with conflict avoidance. To shirk a confrontation because it would be difficult or because I don't like for people to be upset with me is not sufficient or healthy. Peace is hard. Relationships are messy. Participating in difficult conversations is part of what it means to be human and certainly what it means to be people of peace. But when my continued participation in a dialogue or a relationship fuels destructive behavior, in others or in me, then I should remove myself from it, at least for a time.

I don't always know when it is best or right to withdraw from dialogue with others. We should always pray for wisdom in these matters and seek counsel from godly people. In general, however, I have chosen the path of irenic absence when a discussion of issues becomes a personal attack or an attack against my family. It becomes clear in such moments that there is no momentum toward resolution, that the impetus is in the direction of destructive behavior. At other times, disengaging from the conversation is wise because participants have become quarrelsome, squabbling about words rather than advancing the cause of Christ. When listening is not possible, when Christians cannot speak with gentleness and care, when the mission of the church is undermined because of the dispute, the path of irenic absence may be best.

Sometimes the destructive speech comes from people outside our congregations, outside our communities of accountability. In such cases, kind and gentle responses are always appropriate, but disengagement from quarrelsome people may be the best road to peace. In one's own congregation, such a response should come as a last resort. Whenever possible, we should seek active relationships with the brothers and sisters with whom we worship, with whom we sit at table. Moreover, the leaders of our congregations have important responsibilities in this regard. Paul's instruction to elders in 1 Timothy 3 indicates the crucial role they have in protecting the flock from divisive behavior and destructive talk. But whether we speak or remain silent, our behavior should be marked by humility and meekness, patience and love. Even when the attacks are unfair and the accusations personally damaging, Christians act in a Christian way; they maintain the unity of the Spirit in the bond of peace.

I am convinced a further response is necessary, one that may be the most difficult for us to take. We can no longer afford to tolerate, much less support, those who sow seeds of discord among us. However they may rationalize their behavior or characterize their opponents, they are purveyors of unsound doctrine; they are unhealthy teachers. As Paul clearly instructed Timothy, we must have nothing to do with these sorts of behaviors (2 Tim. 2:23). The health of the church is at stake.

We must distance ourselves from those who justify uncivil behavior toward others. Irenic behavior in this case may be to cancel subscription to publications that attack people or that endorse the division of Christ's body. Churches may have to act decisively toward preachers who treat others in ways that do not reflect the attitude of Christ. It is time for the church to love and admonish those whose divisive spirits undercut the witness of Christ in the world, in order that God might grant them a change of heart and lead them to recognize the truth (2 Tim. 2:25). It is time for Christians to embrace those whom Jesus blessed in the Sermon on the Mount as the children of God: peacemakers.

EMBRACING THE PEACE OF CHRIST

Our message has been simple: Christians should be able to talk to one another. We should be able to disagree without hostility. We should be marked by the cross of Christ and known as a people of peace. But we are not. Throughout history, and certainly in our own experience, few Christian qualities have been so rare, so ineptly sought, and so badly needed as peacemaking. As a result, our churches are often spiritually stunted.

The body of Christ indeed is broken. We live in narrow worlds surrounded by people mostly like ourselves. We talk too little to anyone whose opinions differ from our own. We seldom see beyond ethnic and social boundaries. We engage too often in accusation and blame. Each of us bears responsibility. No one is innocent. We build walls of self-protection. We seek our own interests. We do not love as we ought. We are silent when words must be spoken. We shout when everything in the universe calls for silence. Christ's body is broken because we, in our sins, are broken.

In this brokenness, however, lies our hope. Christ's body was broken so that the body of Christ might be healed. He was wounded for our transgressions, as the prophet says. Here is the good news. Our brokenness is met by Christ's. In this brokenness we become one with him and, if we have the courage, with one another. We share in his suffering and therefore in each other's pain. By this means, Christ's peace heals us. It is healing us even now.

In spite of all appearances to the contrary, the peace of Christ is not dormant in our time. Even though many things in our history conspire against it, with all human odds in favor of failure, and in the face of the evidence of fragmentation everywhere, Christ's peace is breaking out. Though some label it apostasy and others call it foolish, though many are indifferent or angry, confused or afraid, still peace is at hand. Often led by our children, who are less sectarian and more fearless than we, who refuse to allow God's grace to be throttled by human religiosity, we see the peace of Christ being embraced. The signs of it are everywhere.

In recent days, two congregations in Texas, who half a century ago painfully divided, met in common assembly, asking forgiveness of each other for past sins, taking the Lord's Supper together as brothers and sisters in Christ. The old differences still remain, but a new spirit prevails. They share what they can in common, including care for the poor and good news to the lost. Here is the peace of Christ.

Leaders at some predominantly white churches and other Christian institutions have offered apologies for the institutional racism that marred our past. While not personally responsible for the discrimination and segregation of another era, they have confessed the sin of their institutions and have repented publicly for the devastating effects of racism. Meaningful conversations are taking place across ethnic lines. Genuine friendships are being formed and fellowship at the deepest level is being extended. This is the peace of Christ.

A quarter of a century ago, friendships were ripped apart and families divided when International Churches of Christ emerged as a separate fellowship. In recent months, many of these relationships have begun to be restored. One ICOC preacher told me that his brother in the flesh, a preacher in a mainline Church of Christ, not only invited him to his home for the first time in two decades but also invited him to preach at his congregation. In the last year I have been blessed to be a part of several meetings in which individuals from both groups came together for the purpose of reconciliation. Each person spoke with candor and grace. With tears and many prayers, they extended forgiveness, each one embracing the peace of Christ.

On several recent occasions, men and women from Independent Christian Churches and a cappella Churches of Christ have met for conversation and prayer. What we used to share in common has largely been lost after a century marked mostly by isolation from one another. No one is willing to compromise what he or she believes to be the gospel. No one is advocating relinquishing those characteristics that have made our respective fellowships strong. But hearts are heavy because of the wounds of our division. No one today is guilty for what happened a hundred years ago, but we are answerable for what we do now. People gather in penitent prayer. As they bend their knees, they confess sin, and each one prays for God's peace.

Relationship between the Christian Church (Disciples of Christ) and the other streams of the Stone-Campbell heritage is more tenuous, for reasons both historical and theological. Yet even here, there are deep friendships and common commitments. Decades of demonizing and caricaturing have had their effect. Real differences remain, of course, differences that will not be overcome if we never speak and never pray together. Similarly, conversations about doctrine are even more complicated with those outside the Restoration Movement who do not share a commitment to the saving work of God in the baptism of believers, weekly communion, and other important matters. I do not underestimate the differences. But those differences will not be addressed if we never talk, if we never listen, if we only view one another through the eyes of condemnation or pity. Here, in spite of all appearances to the contrary, is an opportunity for the inbreaking of the peace of Christ.

Few, of course, will be called upon to address the concerns that transcend an entire fellowship. Mostly, we are confronted by local conflicts—with clashes of personality, disagreements within the congregational leadership, cliquishness, conflicts, and gossip. These, of course, are precisely the wedges that have the power to split churches, and they do so far more commonly than the doctrinal disputes that divide the larger movement. No church is immune. No congregation is invulnerable. The question is not whether conflicts in our churches will arise or whether people will engage in unhealthy talk or destructive behavior. They will. The decisive question is whether we will have the courage in the face of these threats to be a people of peace.

We have choices to make. What we do in the coming days will largely determine who we will be in the coming decades. The future of our churches is being decided now. Will we continue to segregate into groups of people who look and think alike? Will we allow ourselves to be tyrannized by the proximate, blinded by the familiar, seduced by the false promises of Certainty? Will we hide behind the walls of our own making so that we can't even talk to people who are different? Will we grasp the possibilities of our own baptism? Can we offer a place of welcome at the common table of Christ? Can we respond constructively to the fragmentations, large and small, that imperil our churches?

We cannot avoid playing a role in this current environment. We cannot sit out this dance. Even doing nothing plays a decisive role in shaping us because it guarantees that our future will look like our past. How we respond, what kind of people we choose to be, will set a trajectory that will affect the course of our churches and our lives for generations to come. We know, because we are the heirs of those who in similar situations by their speech and by their silence, in ways both constructive and debilitating, shaped our own. We know because God has granted us the grace in our day to be instruments of his peace.

NOTE

1. Frederick Beuchner, *Wishful Thinking: A Theological ABC* (New York: Harper & Row, 1973), 79.

The Door of No Return

My brother how long,
'Fore we done sufferin' here?
We'll soon be free
When Jesus sets me free.
We'll fight for liberty
When the Lord will call us home.

—Spiritual (traditional)

Our friend Samuel drove us on a hot Sunday afternoon from Kumasi in central Ghana to Cape Coast. Early the next morning we made our way to Elmina, the slave castle, in a village nearby. This slave factory was the first permanent structure south of the Sahara built by Europeans. Established by the Portuguese shortly before Columbus discovered the New World, the castle was eventually overtaken by the Dutch and finally the English. By the eighteenth century approximately thirty thousand African slaves were forced onto ships and sent to America each year from Elmina alone. Deportation of slaves through slave castles such as Elmina continued for three hundred years.

A small group of us walked together through cells and courtyards, through stone chambers that once had been so crowded that no slave had had room to sit or lie down. We went into a church inside the fortress whose ministers blessed what occurred within those walls. We climbed the stairs and slipped into the governor's bedroom where for generations and centuries the chief administrators of the fort raped the slave women of their choosing. We were led to the Door of No Return where the slaves had been forced through a small opening onto a narrow walkway leading to the ship where they were forced below deck for the journey across the ocean. For these slaves, the New World was not their destination but some place in the Americas close to hell. The air was still that Monday morning. We were sober as we visualized what had occurred at this place.

Our group listened intently to the stories our tour guide was telling. We all stood together—the descendants of Europeans who had bought and sold human beings for profit and pleasure, the descendants of Africans who had been complicit in slave trading activities by capturing villagers from other tribes or selling to the Europeans the human spoils of their wars, and the descendants of the slaves who had been forced onto slave ships in which many, and in some cases most, did not arrive alive. The African-Americans present that day had traveled from the United States in order to understand something of their story and to connect to their past. We all stood silently, the offspring of those who had participated in one way or another in those shameful events.

The weight of our common history weighed heavily on my shoulders. Everything in me wanted to speak to the African-American family nearby, to get down on my knees and say how sorry I was. But the feelings we all experienced that day were complicated. I didn't want to be patronizing. I didn't want to be cheap. By the time I found my voice, they had moved on.

None of us were responsible, of course, for what had happened centuries before. The decisions of others long dead had shaped a history in which all of us now lived. They had shaped a culture, a way of understanding the world, a way of treating others, that had profoundly affected the way we thought and behaved hundreds of years later. We could not change that history, but we could determine how we would live now.

Edward Ball, the descendant of a South Carolina colonial plantation owner, in a moving book tells his family's story of slave trading and the consequences of those practices in his own life at the end of the twentieth century.[1] Ball interviewed dozens of descendants of Ball plantation slaves, including some who were his unspoken relatives, whose very existence could be traced to the deplorable usage of slaves by their white owners. He eventually made his way to Sierra Leone, in West Africa, the homeland of the original slaves at his family's plantation. He met there a number of people whose ancestry connected them to slave sellers in the area. One woman, Doris Lenga-Kroma, spoke with Ball extensively and sometimes uncomfortably. She could not defend what her family had done generations before. "We must live our lives," she said. "I can't continue to bear the guilt about what my great-grandparents have done. I'll think about it and say, 'Oh, how could people have dreamed such a thing?' I'm born in such a family. I'm not responsible for being born there, but I'm there. What a shame! But what can I do now? What you do with the present is what really matters."[2]

How could people have dreamed such a thing, she asked. But this was the family into which she had been born. What could she do now? What difference could she make now?

These are compelling questions and pertinent to our discussion. We have inherited the actions and words of those who have gone before. In many ways I am proud of my spiritual heritage and grateful for the generations of godly men and women whose lives of character and purpose have so dramatically affected my own. But there are some things for which I am not proud. Some of them have left in their wake a spirit of division. Churches have been split by racist values, by polarizing debates often over marginal points of doctrine, and by powerful and influential personalities. How could they have dreamed such a thing, I sometimes ask. Could they have imagined the instincts toward division that have been left in the spiritual DNA of many churches? Is this what they desired? Did they assume that unkind speech and destructive behavior were normal within the kingdom of God, that such behavior was within God's heart? More personally, I want to know how to respond. What can I do now? Mrs. Lenga-Kroma's words still echo in my heart, "What you do with the present is what really matters."

The past must be reckoned with. It cannot be whitewashed or rationalized. There is an important place in Christian hearts for remembering, and we must not avoid it. But we are living now, and it is now that we must act. We have been shaped by those who have gone before us, to be sure, but we are also shaping our own future and that of the generations to come. What we do and choose not to do will have its consequences, and it is past time that we consider it.

Edward Ball tells of the time he met with Emily Frayer, one of the descendants of his family's slaves, then in her nineties.[3] He tried to ask her forgiveness. She waved him off.

"Forgiveness has to be asked," Ball told her.

"Yes, we forgive," Mrs. Frayer answered. "It didn't hurt me, now, but the people before me, and they all gone."

"We're not responsible for what our ancestors did or did not do," Edward Ball said, "but we're accountable for it."

We are accountable for how we live now. We are not responsible for the divisions of the past. We did not create the climate of racism. We did not choose to grow up in largely segregated churches. We did not participate in the doctrinal debates, write the polarizing articles, or send the email gossip. We are not responsible for a cultural climate in churches that promotes suspicion or argument, cynicism or distrust. Not most of us. But we are accountable for what we do now, whether we are gentle rather than strident, whether we encourage rather than disparage, whether we listen rather than accuse, whether we embrace rather than condemn. We are accountable for what we value, whom we honor, and what we pass on to our children. Before God and to one another, we are accountable.

Some of us are emerging from a sort of slavery, a slavery of the spirit. It is slavery self-imposed, of course, one that emerges from fear or well-intentioned ideals, from cultural heritage or the firm grip of Certainty, but it is slavery nonetheless. Though we may live in ways that blind us to our own bondage, we still need to escape slavery's power. Freedom is what we seek, not merely liberty. The idea of liberty comes from Latin roots suggesting release from bondage, in other words, separation.[4] The word freedom, on the other hand, has different origins. It comes from a Northern European word group associated with friendship. To be free is not so much to be released but to be connected. To be free is not simply to be liberated from something, but it is to be joined to community, to be friends. For Christians, freedom is not doing whatever we want, devoid of responsibility or consequences. Rather, we are free to be in Christ, to be in relationship, to live in forgiveness. We have been liberated from the principle of lawkeeping and from sin, of course. But we have also been freed to serve our neighbor, to love our enemies, to take care of the widows, to provide for the poor. To be free is to belong to a community. It is to be in relationship.

In a world largely suspicious of religious people and institutions, we are free to give without expecting return. In a society balkanized into increasingly narrow political, ethnic, and social niches, we are free to embrace differences. In a culture that prizes retribution and that honors only its winners, we are free to choose forgiveness and to serve and honor those who are last. In an environment in which public rhetoric has become shrill and ridiculing others has become public spectacle, we are free to speak with gentleness and grace. In a social setting that promotes individual rights over the good of the community, that often winks at disruptive behavior and self-promotion, we are free to be disciplined, to be obedient, and to be accountable. We are free to confess, to repent, and to live as if. We are free to receive the kingdom of God breaking into our midst.

We stand before a small portal, a slender gap in the fortress wall. On the other side awaits no cruel master, no slave ship, no chains. Through the opening we see Jew and Gentile working side by side, slave and free walking arm in arm. We see men and women of every social class and of every race committed to a common cause, participating in a common baptism, sharing in a common hope, meeting around a common table, and moving toward a common future. We see a community of brokenness. We see a people of peace. Together we stand before the Door of No Return, and on the other side is Freedom.

NOTES

1. Edward Ball, *Slaves in the Family* (New York: Ballantine Books, 1998).

2. Ball, 435.

3. Ball, 416.

4. David Hackett Fischer, *Liberty and Freedom* (New York: Oxford University Press, 2004).

STUDY GUIDE
& RESOURCE MATERIALS

Jeanene Reese with Gary Holloway

This study guide is designed to enhance the use of the material found in *The Body Broken*. It includes three parts. First, discussion questions for each chapter are designed to assist readers in processing the material in the book and challenge them to deeper reflection and prayer. Second, three congregational scenarios offer readers an opportunity to explore the implications of *The Body Broken* in true-to-life situations. Third, a full case study with teaching notes provides readers a chance to enter real circumstances to discuss issues of fragmentation and brokenness in the community of faith.

Discussion Questions

INTRODUCTION

1. The author asserts that until we address the brokenness of our churches and the divisive spirit that causes it, we will continue to be largely "ineffective in our ministries and impotent in our Christian witness" (p. 3).

   a. Do you agree or disagree with this assertion? Why?

   b. Is there brokenness in your church? What do you think are the possible causes of it?

   c. What has been done, if anything, to heal the brokenness?

   d. What relationship do you see between this brokenness and a divisive spirit?

2. Reese indicates that he wanted to be tender, confessional, playful, candid, and balanced as he writes this book.

   a. Which of these attributes or combinations of them do you think are important for helping us as Christians deal with tension and conflict?

b. What other characteristics do you think are important and why?

For Reflection and Prayer:

1. Reflect on your purpose in reading and discussing this book. What do you hope will be the outcome?

2. If you had to name two to three qualities you would like to grow in through this study, what would they be?

3. After sharing these responses, spend time in prayer for one another.

CHAPTER 1 - HEIRING OUR DIFFERENCES

1. What experiences have you had with the effects of gossip, destructive talk, or divisive behavior?

2. In these kinds of situations, why is it so much easier for us to question the motives of others without first examining our own? What difference do you think it would make if we were more consistent in self-examination and prayer before reacting to others?

3. When do you think it is wise simply to ignore gossip and malicious talk, and when should it be addressed? How do you determine which route to take?

4. Where do you see the effects of division?

a. How do you think it has shaped you?

b. Why is it important for us to leave a different heritage for the next generation? What do you think will happen if we don't?

5. The author identifies four factors that contribute to our inability to discuss our differences. The first three of these are: racism, culturalism, and historylessness.

a. Do you agree or disagree that these have significantly contributed to our difficulty in communication with one another? Discuss each in turn.

b. The fourth factor, and the most influential in the author's spiritual formation, was Certainty. What does he mean by this term? How are his experiences similar to or different from your own? What effect did these experiences have on your faith?

   c. What other factors would you identify as a hindrance to our ability to talk to others with whom we disagree? Why do you think these factors are significant?

For Reflection and Prayer:

1. What experiences in your faith formation have been useful to you in handling communication in difficult circumstances? Offer a prayer of thanksgiving for the religious heritage, personal experiences, or significant relationships that prepared you in meaningful ways.

2. Consider how you would like to impact the spiritual formation of the next generation. What principles would you like to make sure they are given? Spend a few minutes in prayer for young people and the tradition, experiences, and individuals that are shaping them.

3. Examine your life and influence on others. Do you think it is more positive or negative? Spend time in prayer about this response.

For Further Consideration:

For further study on the issues raised in this chapter, see *The Crux of the Matter: Crisis, Tradition, and the Future of Churches of Christ,* by Jeff W. Childers, Douglas A. Foster, and Jack R. Reese (Abilene: ACU Press, 2002).

CHAPTER 2 - SUFFER THE CHILDREN

1. To be God's people is to know both pain and great joy. What experiences can you share that support this understanding of the Christian life?

   a. Why do you think that much of the adversity or pain that Christians have experienced through the centuries come from the hands of brothers and sisters in Christ and not from outsiders?

   b. What effects do you think it has had on relationships among believers and on relationships with non-believers?

2. What evidence do you see of the author's suggestion that the church is not just a sanctuary but also a frontline on which the current cultural wars are being fought?

3. Why is it important, according to the author, for Christians to

determine what they believe in the midst of the current situation?

   a. What do you think are the possible effects of such a careful examination of beliefs?

   b. Which of these effects excite you, and which give you pause?

4. Why is it equally important for Christians to determine how they will act?

   a. Do you agree/disagree that there is often a great disconnect between what we believe and how we behave? Why do you think so?

   b. What effect does our behavior have on other Christians, on the watching world, on our own children?

5. List the reasons that the author believes help explain why young people are leaving Churches of Christ.

   a. What other possible reasons would you add for why young people are leaving?

   b. What would you disagree with on this list?

For Reflection and Prayer.

1. Review the following points made at the close of chapter two. Which of them do you find most challenging and why? Which one poses the greatest challenge to your church or organization?

   a. Our failure to talk to one another when we disagree is a sin against God.

   b. In more than a few churches, truth is pitted against unity, if unity is discussed at all.

   c. We sometimes do not grasp that unity is inherent to truth, that godly accord must not be seen in contrast to good teaching but lies at its heart.

   d. Pursuing peace in not an optional matter for Christians.

   e. Living in unity is not the byproduct of the resolution of our differences.

   f. The peace of Christ is not merely a gift to Christians; it is Christ's witness to the world.

2. Reflect on how these insights shape the decisions you must make about what you believe and how you act.

3. Spend time in prayer about the insights you have gained about your self and your church/organization.

For Further Consideration.

For more insight on prayer, meditation, and other spiritual disciplines that have the potential to heal and bless, see *Prayers that Heal Our Emotions*, by Eddie Ensley (New York: Harper and Row, 1988).

Chapter 3 - Peace and Proximity

1. What does the author mean by "the tyranny of the proximate"?

   a. How does it pose a specific problem for us?

   b. What stories would you share of your own struggles or the struggle of others in adjusting to different contexts?

2. How does the European church the author initially describes sound similar to many churches you know? How is it different? Why is it important for us to recognize these similarities and differences?

3. List the various reasons the author cites for the apostle Paul to write the epistle to the Philippians.

   a. What do they say about his relationship with this church?

   b. Why is it useful for us to examine these possible reasons as well as this relationship?

4. Read the author's paraphrase of the hymn from Philippians 2 aloud.

   a. How does the hymn address the challenges we experience with the tyranny of the proximate?

   b. Why are the other examples of sacrifice Paul gives in the letter—his own, Timothy's and Epaphroditus'—important for the Philippians and for us?

5. Assign these roles—Euodia, Syntyche, the loyal companion, members of the Philippian church—to various participants and ask them to "hear" the author's paraphrase of Philippians 4 as that person. After you read it aloud, discuss the following questions:

a. How did assuming a role for the reading of this text change the way you heard it?

b. Listening from your assigned vantage point, what did you hear Paul saying that you really need to take to heart?

c. If you were actually that person, what do you think would be your first course of action? Why?

d. How do you think the whole church should respond to this situation? Why?

For Reflection and Prayer:

1. Reflect on each of the paragraphs beginning with the question "Do you want to be healed?" in the last few pages of chapter 3. Then answer the following questions:

a. How does conflict tend to rob us of our joy? What do we need to surrender to God in order to receive his joy again?

b. Why is gentleness so difficult when we are struggling with some one? How can God create a gentle spirit within us if we let him?

c. How is prayer an antidote to anxiety? What would change if it became a priority?

d. Why are we so prone to criticize and despise when we disagree? What is so challenging about seeing the best in others at all times?

e. Why is it important for us to recognize that only God can create a way across the chasms in our lives and relationships? What does it mean for the church that the peace of God will guard our heart and minds in Christ Jesus?

2. Spend time in prayer about your response to each of these questions. Ask God to provide the specific healing that is needed in each case.

For Further Consideration:

One of the most difficult concerns in a situation like Euodia's and Syntyche's is how to have the conversation that begins the process of healing. An excellent resource, although not written from a Christian perspective, is the book, *Difficult Conversations: How to Discuss What Matters Most*, by Douglas Stone, Bruce Patton, and Sheila Heen (New York: Viking, 1999).

CHAPTER 4 - CLIMBING THE WALL

1. The author suggests that the play *Fences* challenges us to confront the barriers still visible in our civic life, our churches and our hearts.

   a. What barriers do you see that disturb you most? Why do you think they still exist?

   b. What are the invisible barriers that we often do not see, much less discuss? Why do you think we are so hesitant to see these fences?

2. Reflecting on the polarization that exists in our current political climate, the author asserts that "how people view the truth often determines how they treat those with whom they disagree" (p. 83).

   a. What do you think are the ramifications of this statement?

   b. What factors have led us to this level of polarization in our culture, our churches, and our hearts?

   c. How does our belief "in the inviolability of our own position" keep us from considering the ethics of our behavior?

3. How does the proliferation of churches "of every shape and flavor" hinder Christians from having to deal with our differences? What impact do you think it has on our understanding of discipleship?

4. As you reflect on the high wall between Jews and Gentiles in the ancient church, what contributions do you think each group made to keeping it thick and solid?

   a. In this environment how do you imagine the Christians received the message that Christ is our peace, that he has broken down the dividing wall of hostility, and that he has made them into one new entity?

   b. Why does Paul spend so much time in this epistle talking about the power available to them? How is this message good news to the Gentile Christians? To the Jewish Christians? To us?

5. According to the author, what is the purpose of Paul's description of the sevenfold oneness of Christ in Ephesians 4?

   a. How does this understanding of Paul's teaching impact who we are as followers of Christ?

   b. How does it seriously challenge how we live with one another?

For Reflection and Prayer:

1. Reflect on this statement from *The Body Broken*: "Our task is not to choose our brothers and sisters; our task is to love them. Christ's power is enough to traverse the differences" (p. 100).

   a. What areas do you see in your church or organization where people are having difficulty loving each other?

   b. How would claiming Christ's power in the situation enable you to overcome these difficulties?

2. How would our lives change if we approached every wall "with our hats in our hands"?

3. Spend time in prayer about your relationships.

For Further Consideration:

An excellent resource on coming together as God's people in multiracial congregations is *United by Faith: The Multiracial Congregation as an Answer to the Problem of Race,* by Curtiss Paul DeYoung, Michael O. Emerson, George Yancey, and Karen Chai Kim (Oxford: Oxford Press, 2003).

CHAPTER 5 - SANCTUARIES OF WELCOME

1. Why do you think we are frequently tempted to focus on the externals of baptism rather than its meaning?

2. On a scale of 1 to 10 (1 is strongly disagree and 10 is strongly agree), how would you rate your level of agreement with the author's statement: "If many restoration churches have a problem…it is not that we teach too much about being baptized but that we teach too little about living as baptized people" (p. 106) . Explain your response.

   a. Cite the examples given as evidence of this assertion. Add other instances you think are notable.

   b. What effect do you think it would have on our lives and relationships if we put more emphasis on living as baptized people?

3. In examining Romans 6, Reese states that Paul "is not so much arguing *for* baptism as he is arguing *from* it" (p. 109). How does this view impact our own teachings about baptism?

4. What is the fundamental issue for the church in Rome? What has led to its development?

a. How is this church a microcosm of what is going on throughout the Roman Empire?

b. Why is it significant for churches in the twenty-first century?

c. What difference does it make that God is the beginning of Christian unity and nothing else?

d. What is the significance of the cosmic shift that is occurring?

f. What is the place and purpose of baptism as the new age is born?

5. Why is Paul's challenge for the Roman Christians not to conform to the values of the world but to be transformed by the renewing of their minds and to "present their bodies as a living sacrifice" so significant in light of the unity he has been trying to bring to their lives?

6. Assign the role of Gentile to more than half of the participants and the role of Jew to the rest. Read aloud the paraphrase of Romans 12 and answer the following questions:

a. What does this passage say about how they feel about each other? How they treat one another?

b. How are Christians to deal with their differences? What role does God play in our conflicts?

7. Continuing in the same roles, read aloud the paraphrase of Romans 14 and respond to the following:

a. What does it mean to be weak in this context? How are we to treat those who are weak in the faith?

b. What are the issues in this reading that are dividing the Gentiles/Jews? How does Paul instruct them to handle the matter?

c. Share with the group how assuming a role in this context affected your ability to hear the message of the text.

For Reflection and Prayer:

1. What difference would it make if we were able to disagree without judging each other? Why is it so difficult for us? Pray about the challenges we face in this area.

2. What would it look like if our churches became "sanctuaries of welcome"? In what ways do you see Christian hospitality already at

work in your midst? Pray about the challenges we face in becoming such sanctuaries.

For Further Consideration:

Here are two useful resources on entirely different topics that are both relevant to this chapter. The first is a brief treatment of baptism, *At the River's Edge: Meeting Jesus in Baptism,* by Jeff W. Childers and Frederick D. Aquino, with a study guide by Jeanene Reese (Abilene: ACU Press, 2004). The other focuses on how Christians can discuss sensitive topics without rancor or bitterness: *More Light Less Heat: How Dialogue Can Transform Christian Conflicts into Growth,* by Joseph Phelps (San Francisco: Jossey-Bass, 1999).

CHAPTER 6 - COMING TOGETHER PEACEMEAL

1. How is the author's story of his family reunion like or different from our coming together as the family of God? What can we learn from this illustration?

2. Why do you think eating together is such a significant event in most cultures? What experiences with meals have transformed your life?

3. Examine each of the biblical meals described in the chapter and discuss their importance to God and his people:

   a. The meal at Mt. Horeb (Exodus 24:1-11)

   b. A meal in the last days (Isaiah 25:6-7)

   c. The parable of the great dinner (Luke 14:15-24)

   d. The Last Supper (Luke 22:14-30; Matt. 26-20-29; Mark 14:17-25)

4. How are these meals similar to yet different from the description of the one celebrated each Lord's Day by the early Christians?

   a. What was going on at Corinth that caused problems during the Lord's Supper?

   b. How were these difficulties being manifest in other places in the Corinthian church?

   c. As Paul addresses these concerns he describes two paths that the Corinthians had been taking. What are they and how does Paul respond to each?

d. What is the "third way" to which Paul calls these Christians and, therefore, all believers?

e. What does the term *anamnesis* mean? Why is it significant to our participation in the Lord's Supper?

5. Assign these roles to various members of your group: the wealthy, the poor, slaves, masters, tongue speaker, prophet/prophetess, former idol worshipper, prominent citizen, one who loves to drink, a disciple of Paul, a groupie of Apollos, a loyal friend to Peter (you may devise others from the biblical text). Read aloud the paraphrase of 1 Cor. 11:17-24 and answer the following:

a. What is the primary message you received from this text? Why is it important to the role that you are playing?

b. In this context, what is the role of the Lord's Supper in forming us into God's people? How does our remembering (*anamnesis*) change the way we participate?

6. Next, read the paraphrase of 1 Cor. 11: 23a-34 keeping the same roles, and answer the following questions:

c. What is our response to be as we receive the broken body of Christ in the bread and his blood shed for us in the wine? Why must we examine ourselves as we participate?

d. How should our sitting at table together affect our fellowship with one another?

For Reflection and Prayer:

1. Reflect on the author's assertion that the Corinthian church experienced such internal conflict due to the absence of external persecution and suffering. What might it mean for churches in the United States today? For churches around the world?

2. Meditate on these understandings. Pray for the unity of your church, churches in you region, in your state/country, and around the world.

For Further Consideration:

Come to the Table: Revisioning the Lord's Supper by John Mark Hicks (Siloam Springs, AR: Leafwood, 2002), is an excellent resource for further discussion on the purpose and place of the Lord's Supper in the formation of God's people.

CHAPTER 7 - COMMUNITIES OF BROKENNESS

1. How is fear a "potent emotion that both empowers and inhibits decisive action"? (p. 159) What experiences do you have with fear that illustrates its capacity to empower? To inhibit?

2. The author believes that much of the fragmentation experienced in the church is a result of fear. On a scale of 1 to 10 (1 is strongly disagree, 10 is strongly agree), how would you rate your response to his statement? Explain your rating.

3. If, as the author suggests, all our churches are fractured communities, what obstacles are present? What opportunities are presented?

4. Reese suggests several responses that he thinks are significant in this context. Review and discuss them using the following questions as a guide:

   a. What place does confession have in the midst of our brokenness? What is meant by confession in this context? Why is it often difficult for us to confess to one another?

   b. What does repentance look like as we live in our brokenness? Why is it significant to restoring relationships? To healing wounds?

   c. What does it mean to live "as if"? Why is this principle especially challenging?

   d. What does the word "irenic" mean? Why is "irenic absence" sometimes a loving response to conflict? What are the challenges we face in practicing it? How do you see it evident in the life of Christ?

For Reflection and Prayer:

1. Meditate on what it means to embrace the peace of Christ. What will change in our churches, our homes, our lives, and our relationships with outsiders if we truly embrace it?

2. Outline two to three steps that can be taken towards this embrace in each of the contexts above. Spend time in prayer for each.

For Further Consideration:

A useful resource in determining if, when, and how to deal with personal conflict is, *The Peacemaker: A Biblical Guide to Resolving Personal Conflict*, Updated Edition, by Ken Sande (Grand Rapids, MI: Baker 1991).

Epilogue: The Door of No Return

1. Do you think it is important for us "to make amends" for the past whenever possible? Or should we simply let the past be past? What are the possible ramifications of either of these directions?

2. Reese quotes from Edward Ball, *Slaves in the Family*, "We're not responsible for what our ancestors did or did not do, but we are accountable for it." What does it mean to be accountable for something that you are not responsible for?

3. What do you think the author means when he says, "some of us are emerging from a sort of slavery, a slavery of the spirit"?

   a. What evidence do you see of this form of slavery?

   b. If, as the author asserts, this slavery is self-imposed, why would anyone enslave him/herself?

   c. What is the difference between liberty and freedom? Which is most desirable and why?

<u>For Reflection and Prayer</u>:

1. Reflect on your own spiritual bondage and its origins. Pray for release from the bondage and forgiveness for it. Imagine a life where you are free from this bondage—what does it look like?

2. Reflect on yourself as a freed person, not just from bondage, but for the sake of the Lord and others. What difference does this perspective make in how you live? Articulate one or two freedoms you anticipate living in this next week—pray about them.

Scenarios and Cases

Read the following three scenarios (each is followed by a set of discussion questions). These were provided for use in this study guide by Gary Holloway. The purpose of the scenarios is to draw learners into real life situations that will assist in processing what they have read in *The Body Broken*. Remember that these incidents have no single right conclusion but provide opportunities for individuals to decide what they would do in these situations.

The scenarios are followed by a full case study. A case is a real life situation in which the names and places have been changed to insure the anonymity of all parties. The main task of the teacher in using scenarios or cases is to foster meaningful discussion, highlight significant insights, and assist in examining the ramifications of actions/attitudes. Preparation for teaching a scenario or case demands that the teacher assume a learning stance along side class participants. More, rather than less study, analysis, and preparation are required to effectively teach a scenario or case.

The first step in preparing a scenario or case is to read it carefully, listing the central issues, the main characters, or the major events (any details that help "flesh out" the situation). The second step involves exploring the various paths that a scenario or case might take. The teacher decides on a possible direction and selects teaching tools (role playing, voting, small groups, etc.) that will best facilitate the discussion.

Finally, the teacher will want to prepare a wrap-up of the scenario or case discussion. This task can include summarizing what participants have shared or asking them to list what they have learned. The leader may want to share personal insights about the scenario or case at this point but must be careful not to trump the learning process or invalidate the contribution of others.

Scenario One: Two Halves or One Whole?

For two years, the Park Boulevard church has sponsored an Hispanic ministry. The Hispanic church has met in the fellowship room of the Park Boulevard building while the English-speaking church met in the auditorium. The Park Boulevard elders oversee the Spanish work, but the Hispanic church is slowly developing its own leadership.

Relations between the two churches have generally been cordial, but there have been times of stress. Parking has been a problem. Many times teachers have found their classrooms in a mess after the Hispanic classes. The smell of Mexican food at potlucks has bothered some. There are a few who wish things were back to normal, but most have coped with the changes.

Reba Jackson is one of many in the Park Boulevard church who has become actively involved in the Hispanic work. Reba teaches English in a "Let's Start Talking" format, assists in a class for Hispanic children, and even has had some Spanish speaking families into her home for a meal.

The Spanish work has grown and the Park Boulevard church has declined to where there are almost an equal number in the English and Spanish services on Sunday. Some in the Park Boulevard church want the Hispanic ministry to find its own meeting space. Some want the church to move toward the suburbs and let the Spanish buy the Park

Boulevard building. Some want the church to be one church in two languages, meeting together each Sunday.

<u>Discussion Questions</u>

1. Which of the following options do you think the church should pursue? (Set a time limit in which everyone must make a choice).

   a. They should be one church with two languages. God never intended that the church be divided along ethnic lines. This change would be difficult for some in the English church and some in the Spanish church, but learning new languages and customs for the gospel's sake would be a maturing experience.

   b. To try to be one church in two-languages would drive some in both churches away. For the sake of peace, the two churches should remain separate in the same building-maintaining the status quo.

   c. For the sake of evangelism, the Hispanic church should be separate. They should be given the current building.

   d. For the sake of the long-term members of the Park Boulevard church, the Hispanic church should find its own meeting place. Then things can be harmonious in the church like they used to be.

   e. The church should do whatever the majority of the members, both Anglo and Hispanic, vote to do.

2. Give a biblical rationale for whatever answer you chose as the best option.

3. Could the church do more than one of the choices above? Which alternatives are mutually exclusive?

4. What would be the effect of the choice you made on the English speaking church? On the Hispanic church? On the surrounding community?

5. Is your choice motivated by personal desires, political correctness, rebellion against church tradition, or some other factor?

6. What course of action would you encourage the two churches to take to move toward a decision?

Scenario Two: Divided on the Issue of Unity

Sally and Mike were one of several members of the Washington Street Church that had recently been convicted concerning the importance of working toward unity among Christians. Sally had enjoyed her time in Bible Study Fellowship with Christians from many denominations. Mike had befriended Sam, his Presbyterian neighbor next door. Sam, Alice, and their four children were beyond a doubt the most loving and serving Christians in their neighborhood.

For over a year, Sally and Mike had slowly encouraged the leaders of their church to reach out to other church groups. Finally, they convinced their leaders to join in a yearly inter-denominational Thanksgiving service, even committing to host the service next year.

However, lately they have grown discouraged about the prospects for Christian unity. The majority of the members at Washington Street do not support the interdenominational meetings. Some even think that their church is undenominational and that those in denominations are not Christians. However, for the sake of peace in the church, this group has generally been quiet about their reservations concerning denominational fellowship.

One Friday, Second Presbyterian Church, just across the street from Washington Street Church, burns to the ground in a spectacular fire. Fortunately, no one is hurt, but it will take over a year to rebuild the church. The leaders of the Presbyterian Church ask the Washington Street church to allow them to rent their building on Sunday afternoon, so they will have a meeting place while their building is constructed.

Sally, Mike, and others like them at Washington Street see this as an opportunity to put Christian fellowship into action. Many others at their church, including some leaders, feel that allowing the Presbyterians to worship at their building would be joining them in their errors and would mean compromising essential beliefs.

Discussion Questions

1. What should the Washington Church do? (Set a time limit in which everyone must make a choice from the following options).

   a. They should have a congregational meeting and do whatever the majority thinks is best.

   b. They should volunteer to join the Presbyterians in their worship instead of having a separate service.

   c. They should view this as a chance to show love to fellow Christians, not even charging rent to the Presbyterians.

   d. They should rent the building to the Presbyterians but teach them in hope that they would move from their unscriptural practices.

   e. They should avoid any conflict with the Presbyterians by explaining that it would not be feasible for both congregations to use the building.

2. Give a biblical rationale for whatever answer you gave.

3. Could the church do more than one of the choices above? Which alternatives are mutually exclusive?

4. What would be the effect of the choice you made above on the Washington Street Church? On Second Presbyterian Church? On the surrounding community?

5. What emotion motivates you in your choice? Fear? Pride? Love?

6. Why do you think this situation is so potentially divisive?

Scenario Three: Discerning the Body

Scott and Erica are some of the most thoughtful Christians at Hillside Church. They are "thoughtful" both in the sense of being considerate and of thinking deeply. Recently, they have been especially reflective about the meaning of the Lord's Supper and decided that they needed to give it more personal attention. To remind themselves and others around them of the significance of the Supper, they have begun to say out loud the words, "This is the body of Christ broken for you" and "This is the blood of Christ shed for you" as they pass the bread and the cup to their neighbors at church.

Several have been deeply touched by these actions and not only want them to continue but are hoping that other innovative practices will soon be included in the celebration of the Lord's Supper. A few of the older members at Hillside, however, have complained to the leaders about the practice of Scott and Erica have initiated.

Among the dissenters is JoAnne, a gentle and devout woman who has been a member of the congregation for over fifty years. She and others were taught that the Supper is a solemn occasion when one should focus on the death of Jesus. "I don't like all that talking during the Lord's Supper," she says. "It distracts me." Another member added that "If we're not careful we'll soon be involved in more than one act of worship at a time!"

Discussion Questions

1. What should the leaders do? (Set a time limit for everyone to make a choice from the following options).

   a. Explain to Scott and Erica that they are distracting and offending others, knowing that as mature, thoughtful Christians they will stop their practice of speaking out loud.

   b. Discuss with those who object to what Scott and Erica are doing, knowing that older, mature Christians will tolerate this new practice.

   c. Publicly explain that the Lord's Supper is a solemn time and that talking during the Supper is irreverent.

   d. Publicly encourage all the members at Hillside to be more innovative and interactive in taking the supper like Scott and Erica.

   e. Ask Scott, Erica, and those who object to work out their differences.

2. What is the biblical significance of the Lord's Supper? Does it have multiple meanings in Scripture? If so, what are some of them?

3. Why do you think we often stress uniformity in worship within a specific congregation? Is uniformity desirable in all of our congregations? If so, why? If not, what are we risking?

4. Have we placed too much emphasis on the Lord's Supper by having it each week? What unique challenges do we face because of this decision?

5. What would be the consequences of doing the Lord's Supper "wrong"? What are ways we can do it "wrong" or "right"? What should be our primary focus in celebrating it with one another?

Case Study

A Church for All People?

The heavily accented voice on the telephone was full of anger and hurt: "I have to tell you as my minister how the church has failed me. No one cares that my mother died and that right after I returned from her funeral in Africa, my uncle and an infant niece died. No one except you and two friends came to be with me. Others just called and asked me to do a job. They didn't even express any feeling. They just see me as someone who can work for the church. What is the church for if not to be with you when you are grieving?"

For two years Bruce Derr had been minister of a two-hundred-fifty-member church in a suburb bordering a major east coast city. International organizations and multi-national corporations as well as immigration for political and economic reasons had brought an influx of people to the area from around the world. Seventy primary languages were spoken in the neighborhood high school. The church reflected this diversity; thirty percent of its members came from eighteen different nations.

The challenge of this diversity was the key reason Bruce had accepted the call to become minister of the congregation. Having had experience overseas, he was captured by the church's expressed vision of its ministry: "A Church for All People." A large sign in front of the church building and the congregation's publications made public this mission. The highlight of the year was World Communion Sunday when persons from numerous nations gathered around the communion table in dress from their country, leading in prayer in their own language. He saw this as a foretaste of God's reign where people would gather from north and south, from east and west, and sit at table together.

But Bruce knew it was only a foretaste. He remembered the friction caused by this diversity. Several of the more liberated professional women were indignant at the flirty, macho way Latin American men related to them. At every worship committee meeting there was heated discussion over the hymns to be used in worship. Many of the international folks from missionary backgrounds wanted to sing hymns such as "Onward Christian Soldiers" which they had used in worship at home. But the militaristic tunes and words of such hymns contradicted the understanding of the gospel held by many from a more liberal American tradition.

Those from the dominant culture were quick to express their displeasure in public meetings or through letters to the editor of the church's newsletter. But those from other nations were hesitant to express discomfort with the congregation's ways of functioning except in private conversations with Bruce.

Bruce was pleased with some of the ways lay leaders had sought to deepen communication between persons from different cultures, often incorporating the gifts of each into the corporate life of the congregation. Members from Ghana led worship at the church picnic, involving the congregation in an experience that had been an annual event for them "at home." Forums explored the experience of members from various nations, emphasizing both life in the country of origin and the difficulties of living in the United States.

In spite of some progress in becoming a church for all people. Bruce knew that on a day-to-day basis upper middle class white professionals ran the church. They did business with good process skills and great efficiency. Yet the task was usually more important than persons. He had encouraged the nominating committee to make certain that the diversity of the congregation was represented on the leadership team, an advisory group formed until qualified elders could be appointed in the future, and other committees of the church. The chair of the committee reported back that she had tried to recruit nominees from all the nationalities in the church, but most of those approached had reluctantly declined, stating they worked two jobs and had little time for church activities other than worship.

The telephone call had shattered Bruce's positive feelings and heightened his awareness that the differences in cultural norms and expectations within the congregation were deep and divisive. He knew they had to be named and dealt with. The caller, Ansa, was one of the Africans who had made time to serve on the governing body of the congregation and had been instrumental in establishing a sister congregation in Nicaragua. He could name several members of the congregation for whom Ansa had been an important person in their faith journey.

Although he had a tendency to personalize the congregation's problems, Bruce knew that this was the leadership team's challenge. During the time for sharing of concerns at the monthly meeting of the twelve members of the leadership team, he told of his conversation with Ansa: "She expected the congregation to stand with her in her grieving, and few of us took time to reach out to her. She is angry that people had called inviting her to come to meetings and do things. She saw this as blatant insensitivity to her grieving. She feels her church had failed to meet her spiritual needs."

The leadership team responded with a stunned silence to Bruce's description of the conversation with Ansa. Susan broke the silence, quietly remembering: "Ansa was one of the few church members who called me when I was angry and chose not to come to church for a month. She cared enough to seek me out. It hurts that she feels I failed her." Fred responded: "I need the deep spirituality and concern for marginal people that Ansa adds to our deliberations." But sympathy and concern turned to frustration at not understanding Ansa's feelings.

Ruth, somewhat defensively declared, "When I asked Ansa to do some work on the Mission Committee, I meant that invitation to be a caring way of inviting her to resume activity in the congregation and of re-orienting her to 'normal' life." Ann told of the discomfort she had felt on the death of her father when an African member of the congregation had come to her house and "just sat" for hours. "I felt responsible for entertaining her, and her presence soon became a burden."

Bruce was aware of his own confusion as he watched the self-assurance of the governing body crumble under the honest expression of Ansa's pain and unmet expectations. He was haunted by the theory that was predominant in his denomination: only churches which are homogeneous can be "successful" growing churches. He believed firmly that diversity was a gift of God, and that God called diverse people into community, called them together to be the body of Christ in the world. But was it possible to be "A Church for All People" or were the church growth experts right?

*This case was prepared by Garnett E. Foster and adapted for use here. Copyright (c) The Association for Case Teaching (ACT). All names have been disguised to protect the privacy of the individuals involved. Used by permission.

TEACHING NOTES
Jeanene Reese

A. Objectives:

1. To determine how to minister with compassion and care to grieving people in the midst of confusion and discouragement.
2. To explore the challenges of serving a multi-cultural church in a North American context.
3. To examine the underlying values that form a person's understanding of what it means to be God's people, the church.
4. To discuss the dynamics of power, prestige, and position in establishing leadership at the local congregation.
5. To share theological reflection that shapes and challenges the practice of ministry.

B. <u>Teaching Plan</u>

1. Introduction (15 minutes)
   a. Explain the format of this case: we will process it incrementally, so it should not be read beforehand.
   b. Ask participants to divide into small groups of 3-4 people for discussion. They are to imagine themselves as an advisory group from outside the church to offer personal and professional advice to the minister, the leadership, and the church at large.
   c. Read the opening two paragraphs of the case aloud and ask the large group to identify what we know about the situation at this point. [Ask a colleague to write the facts as given by participants].
   d. Next, ask them to break into their groups and discuss the following: If Bruce Derr came to your small group and asked what advice you would give him as a minister in dealing with this upset individual, what would you say to him? (Remember you have limited knowledge of the situation).
   e. Reassemble the large group and ask for 1-2 insights to be shared from each group. [Write these in another list on the board.]

2. Main section (40 minutes)
   a. Read the next five paragraphs of the case aloud and identify the main issues found there. These will include but are not limited to the following (5 min.):
      1) The church is in a situation where diversity is inevitable.
      2) The congregation seems favorably disposed to embrace the challenges of being a multi-cultural, interracial church.
      3) Some positive actions have been taken to encourage sharing of culture and customs in celebration—World Communion Sunday, members from Ghana leading worship at the church picnic, forums discussing the experience of members from various nations.
      4) Friction is apparent on both a small and large scale:
         • Professional women frustrated with Latino men
         • Missionary hymnody versus liberal American perspective
         • Upper middle class white professionals running church compared to minority members not serving in leadership
         • Resulting focus on tasks, processes, and efficiency versus the importance of people
   b. Read the last five paragraphs of the case aloud and ask the larger group to list the characters found throughout it. Note their

names, their roles, their feelings, what issues they face, and what is at stake for each of them in the current dilemma (10 min.). [Record these on board or post-it].

1) Ansa—the African woman who called Bruce frustrated at the way church members treated her after she suffered the loss of her mother in Africa, her uncle and infant niece in the States. She has taken time to serve on church committees and was instrumental in establishing a sister congregation in Nicaragua. She has nurtured spiritual formation in several members. She is grieved, angry, frustrated and hurt by the insensitivity of others.

2) Bruce—minister at the church for two years, drawn to it because of its vision. He sees the current situation as a foretaste of God's invitation for all to come to the eschatological feast. He knows the good faith gestures made by the church as well as the surface level frustrations. Although he tends to personalize the congregation's problems, he knows the leadership must deal with this one. He is aware of church growth theory and wonders if it is possible to be a "church for all people."

3) Susan—has been the recipient of Ansa's compassion and care when she was angry. Susan is hurt that she has failed her friend in this time of need.

4) Fred—admits his need for Ansa's "deep spirituality and concern for marginal people." But his sympathy and concern turn to frustration when he cannot understand her feelings.

5) Jonathan—defensive and acknowledges that he called Ansa to do work for the Missions Committee hoping that resuming activity would reorient her to "normal life."

6) Ann—speaks of her own discomfort when she was in grief over her father's death and an African member of the church came and just sat for hours. She felt the need to entertain the person and was burdened by it.

c. Next, ask participants to break into their groups again and discuss the following (15 min.): Now that you know more about the congregation and its inner workings, how would your advice to Bruce Derr be the same or different than it was initially?

d. Reassemble the larger group and let each one share 1-2 insights from their discussion (5 min.) When they have finished, ask how their

meeting as an advisory group varied in the two experiences? (5 min.)
3. Conclusion (20 min.): Ask the group to do theological reflection:
   a. What is at stake in this situation? What do you think most
      concerns God? Where do you see God at work? (15 min.)
   b. Brainstorm in your small group: What word of hope or encour-
      agement would you offer Bruce Derr and this church if you had
      the opportunity? (5 min)

C. Suggested Reading

Cunningham, David S. *These Three Are One: The Practice of Trinitarian Theology*. Edited by Lewis Ayres and Gareth Jones. Challenges in Contemporary Theology. Malden, MA: Blackwell, 1998.

Hawn, C. Michael. *One Bread, One Body: Exploring Cultural Diversity in Worship*. Bethesda, MD: The Alban Institute, 2003.

Kujawa-Holbrook, Sheryl A. *A House of Prayer for All Peoples: Congregations Building Multiracial Community*. Bethesda, MD: The Alban Institute, 2002.

JACK R. REESE

THE BODY BROKEN

Audio Edition

An abridged version of this book is available in an audio edition, which includes additional study materials and an author interview on video.

Contact Gaylor MultiMedia
1-615-361-4120
www.gayloronline.com

Jack R. Reese *serves as Dean of the Graduate School of Theology at Abilene Christian University, Abilene, Texas. He has served as minister to churches in Texas, Oklahoma, Missouri, Tennessee, and Iowa. His Ph.D. is from the University of Iowa, School of Religion. He is married to Jeanene, and they have three children, Jessica, Jocelyn, and Jay.*